The Problem Is the Solution

The Problem Is the Solution

A Jungian Approach to a Meaningful Life

Marcella Bakur Weiner
and Mark B. Simmons

Jason Aronson
Lanham • Boulder • New York • Toronto • Plymouth, UK

Published in the United States of America
by Jason Aronson
An imprint of Rowman & Littlefield Publishers, Inc.

A wholly owned subsidiary of
The Rowman & Littlefield Publishing Group, Inc.
4501 Forbes Boulevard, Suite 200, Lanham, Maryland 20706
www.rowmanlittlefield.com

Estover Road
Plymouth PL6 7PY
United Kingdom

British Library Cataloguing in Publication Information Available

Library of Congress Cataloging-in-Publication Data

Weiner, Marcella Bakur, 1925–
  The problem is the solution : a Jungian approach to a meaningful life /
Marcella Bakur Weiner and Mark B. Simmons.
      p. cm.
  ISBN 978-0-7657-0466-5 (alk. paper) — ISBN 978-0-7657-0686-7
(e-book)
  1. Life. 2. Jungian psychology. I. Simmons, Mark B., 1947– II. Title.

  BD431.W2938 2009
  150.19'54—dc22   2009006409

Printed in the United States of America

⊗™ The paper used in this publication meets the minimum requirements
of American National Standard for Information Sciences—Permanence of
Paper for Printed Library Materials, ANSI/NISO Z39.48-1992.

To my family—Dan, Ilene, Laura, Rebecca, and Jason—who all are a blessing in my life.

Marcella Bakur Weiner

To my children, Carrie and Jason, I bestow this story.

Mark B. Simmons

Contents

Acknowledgments   ix

Introduction: Shadow Figures of the New Millennium   xi

1   Fire into Water   1

2   Harnessing the Fire   15

3   Shadow Figures as the Real You   27

4   God as Shadow   41

5   One Plus One Plus One = One Dreaming "I"   49

6   Dancing with Shyness   61

7   Shadow in Relationships   75

8   Depression's Gift   87

9   Shadow Homeopathy   99

10   Dark Angels   111

11   REALationships   125

12   Conclusion   143

About the Authors   147

Acknowledgments

Our deepest gratitude to those who have shared their life processes with us and from whom we learned so much.

To Art Pomponio, former editorial director of Jason Aronson Publishers, whose encouragement and responsiveness was never-ending, our heartfelt thanks.

To Julie Kirsch, editorial director, Jess Bradfield, associate editor, Allison Syring, assistant editor, and Melissa McNitt, associate editor, our gratitude for your caring ways.

To Alla Corey, former marketing manager, whose caring ways and support were always there, we thank you.

To publisher Jason Aronson, now retired, your confidence in us and availability cannot be matched. We are appreciative.

All cases presented have been slightly altered for the purpose of protecting the privacy of those who shared their innermost lives with us.

Introduction:
Shadow Figures of the New Millennium

What comes first? Is the second half of life determined by what happened in the first? Or, is the second half, already imprinted, the determiner of what happens in the first? Are you organized by your fate or your destiny? Jung saw symptoms as meaningful and having a purpose: the reintegration of energies and capacities, pushing toward wholeness, a lifelong developmental process. You get a symptom: a heart condition, a depression, a loss of relationship, a panic attack, a death. The tendency in Western civilization is to perceive this as disease. Jung saw this as a chance for growth and transformation; he believed that these phenomena symbolized shadow—personal and universal energy forms misidentified through culture, socialization, and ego development that are exactly what we need to heal. Jung believed that problems were nature's way of instigating growth and development. In engaging with the shadow personalities and alien energies that demanded his attention, Jung experienced heightened consciousness, an extra layer of awareness that allowed him to participate in the realization of his fullness of being. Contrary to his contemporaries, who made the rational ego the island of consciousness that was the center of the universe, Jung sought a restoration of the connection to the source itself: not the ego but the Self, that Self being essence.

Symbolic of our disconnect from our essence level, we remain stuck in the biblical polarity of blessings and curses—one or the other. A middle path was always available: to "choose life." But the codes, rules, and laws supporting this course have become stereotyped and perverted to the rational ego's fundamentalist black-and-white agenda of certainty, safety, no suffering, intellect, heartlessness, and conflict unnecessary. Without the spirit behind the middle path, being good gets very tiring. Especially when it joins one side of a polarity whose very expression compels the ultimate flip into the other pole. Blessings and curses, Jekyll and Hyde, caught between these extreme poles you lose track because the curses are as powerful and feel as good as the blessings, especially if you are the one doing the cursing rather than the one being cursed. Sometimes, it seems like you need a score card. Plus, being bad feels so good, and vice versa. Have you ever witnessed children running around in joyous, unrestricted ecstasy? Suddenly, you know the laughter will inevitably turn to crying. The other pole is about to hit. This continuum applies to all archetypal experience. The shadow side of the archetype is inherent, flipping from one pole to the other.

What is the third path that resynthesizes these disparate experiences into their archetypal whole? All paths lead to the Self if we follow them by trusting what is happening and consciously going further on the path. In bipolarity, we change our path in a blink, flipping back and forth in a heartbeat. We become masters of not staying on the road. Who needs to go further into depression? Who needs the unnecessary torment to deal with or confront the disturbing individual or problem when there are so many brilliant rational strategies and words available to meet your goal?

Remember that our biggest nature resides in just these disturbances and happenings. That's where the action is. Jung wrote in *Alchemical Studies,* "One does not become enlightened by imagining figures of light, but by making the darkness conscious." Our biggest commandment from nature is participation in the dark experience, going deeper and amplifying the experience, not out of guilt, punishment, repentance, masochism, or secret agenda—but out of "Calling."

In the Yaqui Shamanic tradition, this means becoming your double, your energy-spirit, subtle body, side by side with your physical mortal body. We are an accumulation of wrestling our enemies to the ground to get their energy. That High Dream lives in us, drives us, and creates the problem of our lives that contains our hidden divinity.

The stories of Christ and Buddha mark a manifestation of our high dream nature of Self realization, the natural individual path in each individual's DNA to reveal and embody everything of their nature. The ◄

distortion has been to make this a literal collective lesson, a historical teaching of a miracle, a unique prophesy for the chosen one rather than a symbol of our own personal journey to gain permission to participate in our own high dream. As a miracle, the high dream remains objectified and outside oneself in a form of civilized but devastating idol worship. What if the paradigm changed from worship, rule, and law to active participation in your own high dream? What if our main task is to participate in this great adventure, and what if our task, congruent with our nature, is permission to experiment with relationship, love, desire, and diversity? We must find and live the path of our unique direction, the one that's imprinted, the only one that fits.

"I am the lord your God." "I am the Brahman." "God Is." The rational does not know this realm. It keeps our "I"ness separate, criticizing it, relegating it to the indulgence of childhood fantasy. "I"ness needs the heart. "I"ness is the heart. The commandment infers, Be the "I." Be the "I" of "I"ness. Be the "I" of awareness. Be the "I" of Tao. "I"ness and "Is"ness are visceral—big experiences and awarenesses that the rational mind disavows. The Observer. The Noticer. The Higher Self. He brings the adult. She brings the heart. He brings choice. She brings permission. He/She brings Love. To the field of earth, to our bodies, where its perceived lack is inherent and endemic to our neighbors and orphaned brethren who are hungry for love. Notice. Witness. Sense this ally awaken and relate to the abject deprivation within us. He/she guides us, completes us until our natural connection and order is restored.

As divine beings, we are required by conscious participation to fix our seemingly disparate worlds. Like the rainmaker and the Leper, our individual natural order is synchronized with all of nature. Jung called this connection the Self-ego axis. This natural flow is our nature and drives our High Dream. When the Higher Self in us remains entranced by heaven, we remain alone, forsaken, cheated, unseen, critical, and vengeful. Our Big "I" belongs on earth: awake, aware, and related to our task. We do not get to our promised land collectively. The process is "I." Our Big "I" is the lamp and mirror that lights our world, not from above, but from below. The "I" within us must be realized individually—then reality changes. Each being carries the whole of nature. Each conscious individual lights the universe.

A Guide and Observer is needed to consciously join this process, not nullify it. This the rational delusion: that the symptom or problem is a distortion; that the answer lies outside what is actively trying to happen; that nature is random and discordant from life and what our highest nature wants from us; that what is occurring is not synchronized with our high dream nature, our big "I."

Our path doesn't start at the top. As we see, inheriting the kingdom is the booby prize, albeit the necessary imprinted fate where the old is destroyed and the house we build has crumbled. What happens when we become active witnesses and participants in our own transformation? What occurs when we notice our experiences, images, and our sensory-grounded reactions, take them seriously, and synchronize them to what nature is unfolding? This is our mercy incarnated. Tennyson said, "A man's reach should exceed his grasp or what's a heaven for?" Our heavenly level is right here, not in the world to come but in our ability to feel, imagine, dream, and participate in every experience. We contain all the necessary channels, sensory-grounded attributes, multiple body organs, and centers to hold, notice, and participate in our own alchemical baking.

Jacob knew his battle with Esau was inevitable. He chose to fight on a heavenly sphere. The battle occurred with Esau's angel and did not happen in consensus outer reality. On that conscious dreaming level, the necessary and meaningful experience takes place. The impact is felt. Then, outer consensual reality changes. Jacob is transformed, and the brothers meet in peace. Death can be experienced on a heavenly level.

Imagine finding the symbol of your transformation in your enemy and that you have an existing heavenly level readily available to help you engage your enemy. These participations change reality, change the environment, and change the world. Even if the enemy is a person, a malady, a mood, a resistance, a pervasive environment, or a world run amuck, these enemies transform fate into destiny. These join Self. These make you, You. When the collective literalizes everything, there is no heaven to notice what is going on inside us and around us, no conscious and awake dreaming level that joins what nature is trying to make happen, a new reality congruent with the organism's real desire and essence.

Are you frightened by what is going on? Change is all around. Invaders are at the gates. There is an absence of leadership. Our world is characterized by the worship of the material, a dizzying rate of technological innovation, and unrelenting stimulation and intrusion. We suffer stifling political correctness and provocative abuses of freedom and we uphold the pretense that all is okay and that there is control. We see an increasing disparity between rich and poor and we experience decreasing access to free time, love, and intimacy. The shadows cast against these overt experiences are secretly running the show. To return to the archetypal essence and the High Dream in the background of these experiences, both sides of the polarity need inclusion; otherwise, it's like a continuous election where only one party provides the candidates. The status quo prevails until it explodes. What is not expressed will break through with a vengeance. Engage the shadow now, skip the middleman—identify your own wrestling adversaries and engage them. Beat them to the punch. The world depends on you.

The matter of your subjectivity is paramount. Your shadow and your individual experience is the dream gate to your path and individuation. Do not marginalize your reality. Consciousness is held within each individual, and collective consciousness is an accumulation, the sum of the conscious light that each of us reflects. The light in the world depends on our light.

It's important that we, as a nation, a people, or a civilization, make shadow a personal experience rather than a mob sport. The discourse will change. Who would dismiss or distrust an individual's personal experience when it's genuine? Imagine leaders and people trusting their personal "I" experience rather than relying on the rational pseudo-opinions that are the lexicon of the day. Polarization does not inevitably resolve without participation—and participation starts when you see the disturbing other as your self. An example of unresolved polarization that has reoccurred is exemplified by the opposing views on the Iraqi war. There is very little dialogue but much zealotry, with each side dreaming up the other as the nightmare, literally seeing the devil in each other.

The Right sees the father as worthy of allegiance. The Left sees a boy and a coward who gets away with everything. In Vietnam we saw this kind of polarity prevail. Not only did the 1965–75 protests not bring

LEFT ATTITUDES	RIGHT ATTITUDES
Certainty and Confidence	Certainty and Confidence
Betrayal by the father	Legacy and trust of the father
Conspiracy of the elite	Wealth, class, and social strata
Circumspection, hesitation, moderation	Action
Understanding	Gut
Questioning, no obligation	Loyalty, service, and obligation
Diverse	Focused

the peace one day sooner, they also polarized the nation and achieved the election of Richard Nixon, their arch-enemy who betrayed his promise of peace—all unintended consequences of the fixed position, actions, and absence of dialogue. The status quo prevailed. The cement behind each side's position is the fact that each side projects its shadow on the other. Each side sees itself in the other and despises what it sees and basks in the certainty that it is the other.

During the Vietnam War, each side avoided dialogue. Michael Bechloss released the tapes of President Lyndon Johnson's White House conversations. In the tapes, Johnson clearly expressed his doubts and misgivings about the war. George McGovern said that if he had known about those doubts and misgivings, he and Gene McCarthy, two of the main Democratic senators leading the opposition to the war, would have gone to the White House, talked about it, and come up with a solution. This expresses the nonengagement that exists between disparate poles. Certainly, McGovern was stuck in his position, and he knew, with certainty, that Johnson was his enemy. McGovern came to view Johnson as a powerful father-figure who betrayed and needed to be destroyed. What if McGovern had taken his experience of Johnson subjectively? What if he had wrestled this within himself and used his experience as a guide before he acted out in certainty? What if McGovern had entered into inner dialogue and had it out with his adversary? Would this engagement have revealed a different path or intent? History might have been quite different. McGovern may have been able to move beyond the polarity that existed then (and still exists today).

A main shadow behind the conflict of our times seems to be the father, and everything flows from there. No King, no Father. No King, no Queen, no Mother. No Mother, no Father, no Child. We live in a drunken democracy where Fathers are either untrustworthy, superficial, self-serving, or tyrannical and where Mothers are either unavailable, self-absorbed, unrelating, or martyrs. This results in a sea of precocious, competitive children in the midst of an epidemic of symptoms and diseases that are linked to a failure of early attachment, not unlike what was seen during the World Wars. Maybe we too are at war, don't know it, and don't admit it.

Which brings us to the historical essence behind the terrorist. What is a terrorist? Historically this is a very subjective question—one person's terrorist is another person's freedom-fighter. What we see every day, both at home and abroad, is an added agenda that chooses death and martyrdom over life. Virtually every Western family knows this nihilism from its adolescents and teenagers, who behave as if they have nothing to lose, and from its members who struggle with addictions to drugs or alcohol. What is going on when a fourteen-year-old boy or girl, brought up in a privileged atmosphere, can take over an entire family's dynamic and hold it hostage to his/her death agenda? What is compelling the expression of nihilism, suicide, and murder, not only overseas but right here at home?

Without a King or a Warrior, we have a terrorist and a martyr. The secret is that a terrorist is a Warrior-in-Training and that when we fall into the acceptable bourgeois, rational, material, entitlement, non-threatening stupor of our time, when we disavow our nature for awareness, conflict, struggle, and responsibility, we impel the shadow side of the archetype to appear at the Center, confronting us at every turn to be strong, aware, and courageous. The shadow terrorist becomes the center of action of redeeming our biggest "I."

We have already defined the warrior as that second layer of awareness and attention that we need to carry to negotiate life. Missing detached awareness and involvement provokes terrorism—in the home, in the community, in the workplace, in the nation. The pain of the missing masculine and feminine is so great that modernity has inadvertently supported a cult of nothing-to-lose death behavior. Our secularization has only increased our impulse to act out a tradition of martyrdom rather than rely on inner experience and rites of passage that recognize experiences like depression, conflict, and loss as dream gates for transformation and individuation.

Since we have no rituals or guiding elders to contain these rites of passage, our conscious unconscious brings them to our door in the form of problems and symptoms that exacerbate till they won't be denied. We need to die into life, not die into early death. When the masculine is in shadow, the danger is to project the Father, to hunt down figures who can carry your projection. And your disappointment is ordained. The archetype is split into extreme opposite shadow images, split visions, such as a weak wounded masculine versus a tyrant. We can see from history how easy it is for a tyrant to carry an image of the good father. The problem of only seeing the evil or the greatness in the other is that the Father remains outside yourself. This seems to be where we're stuck. The symptoms of our times bring shadow versions of archetypal essence that appear as horrible people, problems, and symptoms. Next time your renegade teenager challenges your authority, just think, he or she may be doing their job. Compelling you to be awake, aware, and strong, awakening your big "I" that holds the awareness, involvement, and strength that's disavowed in our daily, overcivilized life instigated in your teenager as terrorist so that both of you can be Big and whole. Natural order restores.

How do we know that so-called symptoms, addictions, and disturbing behaviors of the day hold the individual's essence? Because when you trust these experiences, embrace them, amplify them, and wrestle with them, Bigness emerges. Our larger nature reincarnates. For that to occur requires the feminine. The feminine in us is related to feeling and visceral experience. More than that, it's the field in us where all our dreams come together, where all our disparate worlds meet. It's the earth in us, the place where all action and transformation occurs. Without this feminine, polar opposites in us remain split. The feminine allows us to find the essence, that is, the rhythm, the dance between the poles that is ours.

Today, our feminine hides in drama, tragedy, hedonism, and martyrdom. Most of all it hides in feelings. For men who have become predominantly thinking-oriented, feelings have become secondary. Women, who think they are in feelings, are possessed by them. Jung distinguished emotions as the raw energy of nature. He considered feelings to be a rational function. Today, what people usually identify as feelings are mostly emotions. Feelings, the way Jung understood them, are an essence-level capacity to experience distinctions, tune in reliably, and trust experience. The pairing that encompasses our large, masculine nature and our large, feminine nature is in shadow. We yearn for this couple. We expect to see it in our parents. We expect to find it through our mates. Why is it missing? And why are we so disappointed? Why would someone invent this problem? Because the imprint of our wholeness is in us and seeking it outside yourself compels loss and failure.

The feminine dream of feeling, experience, intuition, and love is right here. Owning your shadow as your own, removing its projection from others, and following the process brings the feminine. The essence experience requires both its light and its container. The paradox of feeling is that it needs grounding in awareness and detachment. Feelings, love, relationship, intimacy, relatedness, being impacted, staying present, following the flow of nature are not the province of the meek.
> Like the paradox in AA, you have to be strong to be vulnerable.

To gain control is to lose control. Feelings require this second level of awareness, a consciousness of two separate realities, to be in the here-and-now. In this way, feminine links with masculine and vice versa. A conscious female presence implies a conscious male partner. In that awareness, an inner couple emerges, the inner couple that is in the background of all conscious life and our dreams of relationship.

We have a dream of harmony and oneness in our background. George, thirty-seven, dreams he is at the top of a plateau on a high mountain. To his left stands an eagle. The eagle flies down toward his right and to a woman who is near a ferocious tiger. Everything is peaceful. As he looks around, he sees that animals that should be enemies are paired in harmony. From his vantage, George is awed by this realization. A scene from the biblical Revelation? Or, a high-self experience, an experience of our biggest "I"? We all have this vantage point in our closets, awaiting conscious incarnation. George finds himself an outsider. Could this glimpse from the top of his mountain and this experience actually impede his daily life and make him depressed? Yes. Because his mountain view and his eagle belong on earth, in engagement with daily life where opposing realities need engagement to reveal their essence. This takes work, and participation, not seclusion. To give up a heavenly perch and to involve our biggest "I" in our forsaken journey heals the split between our heaven and earth. Until George embodies his big "I" dream as an ally, by noticing from this perspective and by guiding himself from this, he will remain eternally alone in his outsider role. Ironically, when he takes on the energy of the insiders and those who exclude him and when he amplifies this shunning energy, he unfolds his own big "I."

With consciousness, all paths lead to the Self. Without consciousness, the big "I" remains in shadow on top of a mountain, not related to our suffering. And George's role as outsider/victim is entrenched. As we identify with our Big "I," we grow and accumulate. There is no finality. The process is more desire, not less. The feminine, which is body, feeling, love, and inclusion, is the container for our fire. Until then, our high dream remains in shadow, sought, even hunted, but outside our Self.

Entranced in looking for the Great Mother, Father, King, Queen, Feminine outside one's self rather than from within, we remain stuck in the loneliness of our absent Higher Self ally. In the West, the High Dream takes on a messianic vision. We hope the Messiah will come. This makes a literal image of a process that's occurring in us. Jung called this process Individuation, which encompasses the conscious inclusion of all our nature, pushing our unique direction and path guided by our problems which hold our hidden nature. The process takes us from the "I" that is God and not us, to the Big "I" of Individuation, where the organism realizes its full expression. Then you are YOU, and the problems of your life that retarded your progress become actualized wellsprings of accumulated energy and consciousness now lived.

CHAPTER 1

Fire into Water

INTRODUCTION

Why Jung? Unlike his contemporaries, who focused on man's capacity to achieve a rational island haven in a random and unpredictable universe, Swiss psychoanalyst Carl Jung chose to trust and follow nature. Nothing is random. Nature is ordered; there is intent and purpose. Behind all manifestations, the problems and symptoms of our lives are organized by intention. The problem is not to be solved by overcoming one's nature, but by joining it.

Believing that we each live in our own uncompromising way, he was aware that this also meant upsetting people. "To be normal," he said, "is the ideal aim of the unsuccessful." For Jung, truth exists where the exclusively rational attitude of human psychology is replaced by each of us going our own way, ever conscious of the loneliness that may be intrinsic to this.

The following chapter details the concept of Jung's *individuation*, its search, its abandonment, and its consequences. It also looks at his basic concept of the realization of the *Self*, the state of higher consciousness, when it is recognized and when it is ignored. Case studies, taken from our clinical files, are altered in some details to protect privacy and are offered to you, the reader, with the premise of this book: that problems do, indeed, hold our solutions.

A ONE-SIDED IDENTIFICATION

As a little girl Lucy loved stories. She read them, she drew them, she told them, she understood them. By the time she started school, she was already known as the greatest storyteller in her neighborhood. A natural, she had a story for every subject, problem, and human event. If she didn't know one she made one up.

Yet, Lucy's teacher at school did not seem fond of her or her storytelling. She wanted the work done her way, the school's way. She told Lucy that she did not like the way she worked, the way her mind "wandered." She chastised Lucy in front of the class. Lucy felt shame for being criticized and singled out, but she hid how bad she felt from the teacher. She came home forlorn. Then she saw a sad-girl face in her bathroom mirror and began making faces. She noticed a face in the mirror that was suitable for school, an earnest and pleasing face that looked interested in what the teacher had to say.

Lucy decided that from that day on she would bring this face to school. All day Lucy would pretend to fit in, to like what was going on. Then, as soon as she got home, this face would come off and she would be herself again. Lucy succeeded beautifully. Now teachers and parents alike knew what a good student she was. Lucy basked in the glory of her admiration and acceptance.

One day Lucy came home from school and forgot to change back to who she really was. The school face became her face. The stories were discarded in favor of school projects, television, and social activities. Lucy's adaptation was completely successful. It wasn't long before only Lucy's mother remembered her as the greatest storyteller in the neighborhood.

What happened to Lucy's story nature? Where is the young, intuitive and exuberant soul who never forgot to take off her mask? Now that Lucy fits in so well, the pain is horrific. In her forties, life rushes by without meaning, substance, love, or risk. By society's standards, Lucy is very successful. But there is no longer any energy or joy in her success; the safe harbor of her adaptation is now an albatross. We become socialized fast, our nature flooded by water, which takes the shape of its container.

WHEN CRUMBS ARE ENOUGH

Angie has achieved national renown as a corporate communications and organization expert. Young, beautiful, and powerful, she captivates an audience. In her professional role, she really looks like she has it all together. Awake, aware, and alive, she performs. But in the intimacy of her home she is a completely devastated, barely functioning woman. The split between these experiences is so wide, so compartmentalized, that when she is performing professionally, she is not aware of her devastation. "When I'm at work, I'm totally there. The audience and I are one. I'm found. Then I go home and cry."

Angie is more closely identified to the corporate "I." This is who she thinks she really is: energized, competent, secure. Who is this other devastated woman? "Why do I stay married to such an abusive, unloving, and distant person?" Angie wonders fleetingly, the question an envelope never to be opened.

ENTER THE SHADOW

Maybe you know someone like Angie, an American success story secretly entombed. What is being played out here? Since Angie embraces only her competent, worldly self, she can't understand how scared, vulnerable and dependent she really is. And she knows it's her fault!

Secret players in this drama:

A young girl is caught in feelings of fear, devastation, abandonment, and martyrdom. Expectation of love and caring never fulfilled, she feels orphaned, with no ally, no mirror. She feels no permission to take or receive, just an instinct toward survival. Who is she? It's our young, traumatized Angie, who never grew up, who is never noticed in the whirlwind of her achievement. She is an outsider to the tribe's collective opinion, driven by all the "shoulds" and "supposed to's," to fit in and succeed, to be extraverted, driven, and aggressive. A criticism of all feelings, intimacy, and real connectedness, everything that young Angie yearns for, does not exist. She feels no self-acceptance. What prevails is a perfectionism that rationalizes the status quo, that colludes to keep things as they are. Intertwined in Angie's façade of success are fixed images of the past: early childhood, family, siblings; pervasive emotional atmospheres that screech relentlessly in her like a plane never to land; a one-sided overidentification with inflated, grandiose, exhibitionistic energies, as if they are the real Angie. This betraying, self-alone self is unreliable, immature, selfish, unrelating, and sadistic, lived out in the actual marriage relationship and the image of her husband.

What is the instigating force behind this drama? Do the spell-like repetitive reenactments hold a secret essence? Do they have purpose? Yes. Our problems are ₁purposefully organized around our hidden essence, which is the paradox of individual growth. That problems contain their own solution sounds unreal to the rational mind—the part of us that stays outside the fray, that does not let our contradictions collide. Problems? What an opportunity! The problem brings the second reality, the necessary counterforce to our first reality, our rational mindset. Our hidden truth includes the simultaneous presence of both realities: society's "shoulds" versus who you really are.

What is the hidden truth in Angie? Night after night she comes home and shuts down, her words childlike: "I don't want to, I don't want to." Three hundred thousand "I don't want to's," three hundred thousand autopilot shut-downs with no meaning or redemption. Awareness can sense or intuit the hidden energy in the shut-down. For Angie to experience the energy of her own shut-down, she must plunge into it, catch its direction, attach to its movement, like the wave you must join in order not to drown. Then the spark hits.

It sounds simple, so why can't people do this? Because it's our belief that it's wrong to have problems, that having problems means there is something wrong with me. But unlike the dust on our coat, problems can't be brushed away. Problems return us to our most traumatic moments. Is this nature's conspiracy, or are we returning to the moment of our wholeness, to the very resource we need? But who volunteers to go there? We survived once, so now the problem is the devil we know. Facing our problems requires leaving the certain world we know and identifying with seemingly alien forces, trusting that what is happening has a purpose. However, this demands the work of higher awareness and the tension of combining two or more opposing, contradictory forces. For example, in Angie's case, we have a super-successful high-achiever by day and a depressed, undeserving victim by night. Who is the real Angie? She is the sum of both.

What did unfolding Angie's shut-down reveal? It sparked the fire of her desirous nature. "Mine," she enthusiastically yelled. The truth of her shut-down behavior is her "me" and her "mine" instinct, her right to get and take in this world, her right to have a "me." Every time she shuts down she secretly takes. The initial shut-down was born of a fire for survival, a fire that was too dangerous to express openly. There was no mirror for this fire. It wrapped itself in clothes of shut-down ritual, her secret "me." Martyrdom, victimization, dependence, depression. The secret "I"s of our generation stuck in daily tragic and destructive "me" dramas, the small *self*, which refers to the ego or personal, and Jung's *Self*, which transcends the ego and inheres the age-old capacities of the species, its goal being wholeness.

"I am the Lord, your God" reflects the Self, the bigger "I," a state of being, a here-and-now presence, an incarnation of totality, a field in us where all worlds come together. "Man," said Jung, "cannot stand a meaningless life." Where does meaning come from? From an affirmation of the Self. Passionately on the side of individuation, the Self, our bigger "I," seeks growth and development of our lives. Contrast that with a smaller "me" that seeks an island of control and survival at any cost. "Me" remains unmirrored, alone, and completely identified with the prevailing state of being. "Me" is always seeking its mirror. Conscious "I" is the result of a witnessed and reflected "me." How does an unmirrored "me" find itself? By compelling its own destruction by forces and realities it has disavowed.

Angie's experience of her desire returns her to the flow of her nature and the path of her heart. She now has choices; moreover, she realizes her big secret: that her shut-down drama holds the spark of her nature to receive her "I." Higher awareness, attention, and witness require being in two realities at the same time. Ancient teachings are always presented in argument, dialogue, or hidden paradox. Real truth exists when there is a tension of opposites, a necessary polarity where a third reality, the hidden truth, can emerge, be experienced, and be welcomed.

DRIVING OUR DUAL NATURE

In Plato's *Phaedrus* there is an image of two horses, a white horse who is obedient, docile, and in complete service to our higher spiritual nature versus the black horse, easily distracted by passion, personal desire, and rebellion. To Plato, these horses parallel the dual aspect of our nature. In order to harness these seemingly contradictory forces, we have the Charioteer who brings awareness, purpose, and skill to driving our horses, harnessing our life/death energy so that our chariot moves forward. Though seemingly oppositional, these two horses represent one reality. It takes a conscious driver to use the two of them purposefully.

Ancient myth, tale, and practice see the enemy as an ally, to be wrestled to the ground to get its energy. Today we have forgotten the need for this struggle; we glorify nonstruggle, revering political correctness and deliberate avoidance of conflict, and contradiction. By colluding with the collective ideal, we invite our own destruction.

THE SHADOW AS ALLY

Thomas, a thirty-four-year-old male, presented a frightening, recurrent dream he had throughout his early childhood. In the dream, he was alone at home. A frightening large Satan-like figure would know wherever he was in the house and would appear there. The figure would always be waiting for him wherever he ran. As a child, Thomas had been witness to many incidents where his father sexually abused his older sister. Despite his seeming ability to throw off the effects of the experience, Thomas remained traumatized and stuck in feelings of helplessness, guilt, and pain. He felt he was living a lie.

While these frightening dream figures are often allies, who has the courage to engage them? Thomas did, by taking over the expression and the movements of the Satan figure. He began by standing and gesturing just like the figure in the dream. Gradually, he took over and embodied the movements and expression of the dream figure until he did not know the difference between himself and the figure. It was at that moment that he felt strong, adequate, and protected—for the first time. He connected his feelings with the figure's energy and intention, experiencing that the figure was there to support him, protect him. At thirty-four, Thomas could now use this energy, this awareness, consciously. He is the warrior who goes into the unknown and stays conscious. What initially appears to us as a frightening and destructive shadow figure may have life-preserving qualities.

STRUGGLE REWARDED

Jodi, a forty-three-year-old woman who had struggled for sobriety for several years, suddenly had a dream that she was on an elevator that took her to the basement. There she met a successful man whom she had known earlier. He embraced her, told her that he loved her and totally accepted her, and promised that he would be available whenever she needed him.

Now she has an elevator that moves up and down; she is no longer stuck on one floor in one fixated mindset. Dreams are sent to us for one purpose: to give a message, carry the meaning of our lives. Jodi is now on an elevator, which contains movement. We push a button and can go up or down. This means that the flow of Jodi's nature is back, that she is no longer stuck in one addictive state; that she can see the world from different perspectives and access various feelings and capacities. Notice the supportive nature of the masculine figure. Imagine what kind of a man is there when she's stuck in her addictive mode. This type of man indicates change. In this pairing with her inner masculine supporter in her dream, she is not the woman who used crack. Since this occurred in the basement, just below the surface of daily life, conscious effort can bring this subterranean experience of inner acceptance and support to everyday life. To retrieve this experience from within rather than seek it outside yourself, by attaching it to an outside person, is the ongoing battle.

It's easy to engage in pseudo-war. We think we know the good and bad parts of ourselves, but we have no rituals in our current culture that support conflict with these seeming opposites. A real secret emerges when we engage in this kind of inner war, an essence is encountered—a new experience of oneness. We eventually realize that there is no contradiction in our opposites, no clash. The opposites have oneness, no conscious polarity. Only in being one or the other do we remain polarized. The existing order will always prevail when we remain in polarity—nothing new will ever happen. When we avoid the clash between our seeming opposites, we don't enter the dance that exists between the two poles. By staying split we remain in the certainty of who we think we are, forever yearning for essence.

Being good and compliant, being selfish and hedonistic, is the same drunken trance, a secret partnership, one unaltered continuum. For Jodi, being good gets tiring, so she drinks excessively. This is a familiar and repetitive drama. In identifying with one side or the other of our being, we remain unconscious, entranced, asleep. Every neurosis, repetition and addiction has its secret gratification. The ego, which is who we think we are at any given moment, is secretly married to the Personal Shadow. Personal Shadow figures ruthlessly collude with the rational ego: lying, rationalizing, threatening us, making us distrust our dangerous truths and return to the certainty of the established order. "Why suffer?" Concerned family, friends, and counselors pop up in this role.

Ryan was forty-seven when he dreamt that he was in the subway and the voice on the loudspeaker summoned him to go to a certain place. When he got to the designated location, he found a sickly man full of AIDS aggressively demanding that he get closer and massage his prostate. In actual life, Ryan had spent many years looking for a father-mentor. He had lost his own father at the age of ten and was envious of what he thought everyone else had. Over the years, he attached himself to several undependable, stealthy business partners. He pursued these men with great devotion and sacrifice, unabashedly attributing all the excellent characteristics of his ideal mentor-father to them.

Often he wound up supporting them when they didn't pull their weight. In reality, these men more resembled the character of his Shadow. Figuratively, Ryan had massaged a lot of prostates. To meet a Shadow figure like this is not pleasant, but it really brings the secret behavior and desire to the light of day. This is the vulgar nature of the Shadow when it shows up. The figure also contains Ryan's deep desire and ability to take for himself. But this was contaminated.

There is a bright side: with awareness, Ryan's desire does not have to live in Shadow. When connection to his Self is established, Ryan's natural instinct to receive is redeemed. Find the path of your true nature and unfold it. Swiss psychoanalyst Carl Jung called this *Individuation*. We're used to a pejorative view of the Shadow, but Jung said that the Shadow "is at least eighty percent gold." We project our good stuff onto others, held there until we are compelled to redeem it for ourselves. Our strengths, capacities, and hidden natures are entangled in the image of others, where their orchestration in our lives brings us face-to-face with ourselves. The dramas of our relationships carry the larger story of everything we really are. The dimensions of what our encounters hold are a life's work. In Ryan's case, his real desire, his permission to get, to receive, to have a life, was held in the image of unstable, selfish father figures.

One implication of Ryan's story is that you can work on any relationship by yourself. What looks like a disturbing attribute in the other reflects something in yourself. Only by embodying this trait yourself, only by joining its energy, feeling it, finding its movement, its song, its rhythm, only by holding its gesture, can you begin to feel and unfold your own essence that is hidden in the other's image.

SHADOW REVEALED IN FAMILIAR PROBLEMS

Stephanie, a twenty-two-year-old female law student, said that since she was a little girl she always measured herself against others and came up short. Now that she is in law school, she says that she always "tries," with a modicum of success, but that she never can get "over the wall" the way other people do. Other people have no problem getting over that "wall." As she spoke, she demonstrated with her hands the sudden interruption of forward movement when she reached the "wall."

The "wall" would always appear when she was challenged or tested. When she expressed this reality, Stephanie's voice was young and incongruous with her law school student age and identity. Here is a perfect example of how the problem, how the symptom, brings the Shadow's gift and why Shadow work is spiritual. From the ego's vantage, the "wall" is a problem to be overcome. From the Higher-Self's vantage, the "wall" is a Shadow figure and energy storehouse that will naturally appear as its energy is needed.

What does it mean for Stephanie to tap into her "wall" energy? She must be like her "wall" as she describes it: stand strong, stiff, tall, wide, unmovable, eyes open, with granite blocks at the bottom, unceasingly and naturally supporting weight. "When God gives you lemons make lemonade." In the Shadow journey, when God gives you a lemon, be the lemon. How can Stephanie incorporate the "wall?" By being the wall. How did Stephanie access the wall's energy in the moment?

First, through her hand movement, which felt the wall's immediate boundary and strength. Then by physically joining its strength, solidness, and immovability, connecting to its attitude and intent. Then, by using it to solve her biggest problem, not by thinking but by walling. For Stephanie it is "walling." What happens when Stephanie "walls"? She stays centered, focused, strong, grounded. Her mind is clear. She's no longer vulnerable. She feels her feet. Operating from a much slower rhythm, she's actually twice as fast. And it shows.

For Thomas it meant being "Satan-like." Think of what your disturbance looks like. Now, *be* that disturbance. See it, feel it, move it, until you become it. And notice the inevitable demand to stop and return to the safety of the familiar.

The "wall" is Stephanie's second reality, grown up, detached, conscious, which can choose and say "no." This figure and energy must be identified with and used. Otherwise, it remains in its Shadow state, free-floating, disidentified and troubling to a fragile identity, rather than being one's inborn endowment. Stephanie's "wall" voice is now fully grown, and she has taken her place as successful lawyer who has no trouble competing with the brilliant minds of her profession. This is the "I" of Shadow. Trust, don't discard, images, symptoms, and problems. Regard them, cook them, and bring them movement. Amplify them. Be them. Find their energy, their intent. Use them, feel them. Let them talk. Be the witness, the noticer, the experiencer. Be here. Be aware of the anxiety, fear, criticism, and guilt at the edge of using this new energy-insight.

Like Stephanie, there is another "You" lurking in your problem. Not the "you" you are used to. Not the "you" you ordinarily see with. Not the "you" everyone has applauded. Not the "you" of your rational mind. The problems and symptoms of our lives bring the possibility of other dreams, other mindsets. They indicate new energies, loves, capacities, paths, and missions waiting to happen.

At the gate of entering these new dreams stands the rational, collectively driven "you," the one you know best: judging, criticizing, accusing, colluding to protect the status quo. If you dare enter the dream of this other "you," you will be outnumbered. Ancient wisdom understood that before entering the gate of the new dream, the rational "you" must have its say. On Mount Olympus, the Pantheon of Greek Gods would meet and make plans for mankind. Before implementing their plan (dream), they always gave space to the Goddess Nemesis to have her say. She would criticize the plan and tell them everything that would go wrong. By this expression, the dream gate could be entered. When Nemesis wasn't consulted and when her expression would not occur, she would exact vengeance and sabotage the dream. This is the role of the rational "you" at the dream gate. The circuitry for the flow of the new dream depends on the conscious expression of this resistor.

Fortunately, the gate of entry to the other "you" is marked by problem, pain, and symptom. Otherwise, we are so addicted to our familiar status-quo survival adaptation that we never notice the other aspects of our nature unless they reach compelling expression. For example, take depression: Why would anybody in their right mind voluntarily enter depression? Why would anybody embrace it? Wouldn't that lead to more depression? "I must be doing something wrong." "It's an illusion, a failure in me." "Suck it up." "Move on." Furthermore, we have no modern rituals and rites of passage for processing this experience and no spiritual teaching of seeing the enemy, in this case depression, as an ally—or the enemy as our Self.

There is a higher self-essence level in each of us that appears at the dream gate. Remember the rabbit that appears to Alice in *Alice in Wonderland* right at the point of entry to the unknown? At first, Alice rejects following the rabbit's invitation. She verbalizes her fear and her desire to stay in the familiar. The rabbit enters, then returns. This time Alice joins the journey with her rabbit (an aspect of her Higher-Self) as her guide.

Our culture emphasizes a requirement for and entitlement to immediate amelioration of pain. We demand it from others as well as ourselves: "Get a life." "What's wrong with me?" "Everyone else is fine."

"I'm defective." "I need to be comfortable." This mindset prevails to the point where Shadow bursts forth, not to be denied.

The alternative use of our awareness is to notice our symptoms and tendencies as doorways to our nature. The real spirituality is to realize that everything comes from within, that our experience is nonlocal, that you contain the other and the other contains you. The next time you see a depressed person, know that in yourself. What attracts your notice of that depressed person is a piece of yourself, now attributed to the other. It takes one to notice one!

Debbie, a forty-three-year-old woman stopped using drugs seven years ago. Sometimes, in times of stress or challenge, she dreams of crack. Conventional wisdom would see this as a literal desire for crack, a regression to her addicted self. For Debbie, crack supported a very strong, assertive, taking-for-herself part of her personality. She would dream crack dreams synchronized with events that required her to be strong, assertive, and concerned for herself. For Debbie, this strong part of her personality is symbolized by crack. Over the years, Debbie has become tougher, more expressive, and assertive in recovery. By sacrificing using crack, she has learned to use the energy, toughness, and alert state that she experienced with crack in life.

WRESTLING WITH THE SHADOW TO GET ITS ENERGY

One biblical story unfolds with Jacob, in collusion with his mother Rebecca, tricking a blind Isaac into bestowing the legacy on the second son, Jacob, instead of first-born Esau. Isaac's blindness, seen from its deeper meaning, refers to inner-seeing. When Isaac became blind as a result of being sacrificed on the altar by his father Abraham, it meant that his own desire to receive for the self was sacrificed and that a new, deeper perception from humility and awe burst forth. His rite of passage incarnated introversion, humility, and the profound reality of inner experience. He and the world would never be the same. Through humility, through feeling his wound rather than acting it out, Isaac made room for the divine.

Eighteen years in exile had prepared Jacob for his ultimate battle with his avowed enemy-brother, Esau. On an outer level Jacob had restricted his inner Esau for eighteen years. Jacob had long abandoned Esau's clothes, the outer garments Jacob wore when he tricked his father. When Jacob was returning to the land of his legacy, he was notified that Esau was coming after him with four hundred men on horses. Jacob divided his camp into two, creating a tension of opposites, and went to spend the night between the camps. A dark stranger came and they engaged in a life-and-death wrestle. At daybreak, the stranger had to leave. Jacob would not let go until the stranger renamed him "Israel." Who was this dark stranger?

When Jacob divided his camp in two, he made room for this other. The stranger has been called Esau's Angel, but he is more than that. It was important for Jacob to incorporate Esau consciously; Esau is his other half. That Esau had four hundred horsemen is indicative of the life energy that Esau contained, that Jacob needed to be whole. The four hundred horsemen indicate the connection between heaven and earth: "As above, so below." That Jacob would wrestle with this entity at that central, sacred moment means that not only was this an engagement with Esau, it was an engagement with the Self, with God. Why does Jacob participate in this battle? Because Esau is the center of the action for Jacob: Esau is the where God resides.

The experience altered Jacob as evidenced by his change of name to Israel and by his wound. Until then, Jacob was just a higher soul. Now all his preparation, work, and love could live in the here-and-now, in relationship and in community. Jacob understood the connection between inner and outer events. By doing the inner work of inner war, he became whole, and his brother greeted him in peace. Israel is the revealed third—greater than the sum of Jacob and Esau and connected to the Self. We can't avoid the imprinted experience. To work with our own Shadow is equivalent to wrestling with our own dark stranger to get its fire and make it our own.

CHAPTER 2

Harnessing the Fire

"Thy fate is the common fate of all. Into each life some rain must fall."

—Henry Wadsworth Longfellow

Throughout his long life, Jung remained a deeply introverted man, more interested in the inner world of dreams and images than in the outer world of people and events. From childhood, he possessed a genius for introspection—experiences of which the great majority of us remain almost completely unaware.

In this chapter, we focus on the Jungian concepts of the hero/warrior and shadow and dreams. These ideas are further developed through discussion of examples from our case files, which have been slightly altered to adhere to standards of privacy.

Where is our fire? It's there at birth. What is born? A desire to receive. Where does it come from? Our empty space, our inborn lack. From our first cry we know something is missing. What is missing? God's image. Where is it hiding? Within us. Where do I find it? You must retrieve it. How does this happen? By choosing to embrace your problems as your guideposts and seeing them not as random events but as markers. What happens when you leave the safety of the tribe in search of the Self? You find your fire. You live your journey. The healing realization is that this world is created for us. "The world's a stage," not to perform but to receive. Then the spell is broken. What spell? That I am alone. That life is meaningless. That I am my wound. That I need permission to live the fire of my true Self nature.

How did the idea of Self (with a capital S) come about? In 1918, following the Armistice, Jung served as commandant of a camp for British internists. His duties included working on a series of drawings that seem to express his psychic state at the time. He soon realized that these drawings resembled ancient mandalas, primordial images of wholeness. Although circular, they incorporate some representation of a cross or a square. Their center contains a reference to a deity. Jung understood this as representations of the Self, the central nucleus. He found that these drawings enabled him to give objective form to the psychic transformations that he underwent each day. In time, he acquired through them a living conception of the Self.

Jung said that the spark of life is born in the darkest spot. By accessing our own death spot we find again the rhythm of our nature and our path. We join the flow of life. The warrior says, "Today is a good day to die." We say, "Today I will be alive, I will be awake. No pity. No self-importance. No attachments to hold on to." We access our death spot every time we enter the dream gate and stay awake.

For the male, the death spot is confronted in the symbolic stories of the hero myth. Here the hero leaves home and is subjected to a number of tests ending in the supreme ordeal of a fight with a dragon or a sea monster. Triumphant, he is rewarded with the throne of a kingdom and a beautiful princess as his bride. To embark on this adventure of life, a boy has to first free himself of his bond to his family and win a place for himself in the world, the kingdom. To do this he must overcome the power of his unconscious mother complex in order to fight with the dragon. This involves the severing of the umbilical cord, in a sense dying as his mother's son to be reborn as a man worthy of the princess and the kingdom.

In girls, the transition to womanhood follows a different path: since feminine consciousness does not demand a radical shift of identification from mother's world to father's world as it does in boys, there is no rite of passage. Instead, the task of bringing new feminine consciousness into being falls to the initiated male. Typical of this are the myths and fairy tales in which the heroine lies sleeping until a prince comes to waken her with his kiss. She is the Sleeping Beauty or the slumbering Brunnhilde awaiting the arrival of her Siegfried.

BORN AS FIRE

We're born as fire. We get hurt by our fire. It becomes dangerous to be the fire that we are. It becomes our secret, that we care, that we feel, that we are passionate and heartfelt, that we are angry, that we are hurt. These images represent inevitable burn by our own fire. In the fire of survival, we forget our original essence and that our initial adaptations were born of fire. But we soon become overidentified with our adaptation and come to believe that we *are* our personality mask. We forsake the part that our fire essence plays in our survival and only relate to the trauma and outer form of our adopted behavior and beliefs. We neglect the fire that brought us here, our initial heroic instinct.

There is an important distinction between Hero and Warrior. Heroes die. Warriors live on. The earthly hero in us is a fighter who withstands ego's onslaught against wholeness. The twelve-step programs say that "fuck it," is the addicts' mantra. The irony is that the same "fuck it" can be used heroically. When we face our challenges and literally fear for our life, we need a "fuck it" in our repertoire. Conversely, it's hard to always struggle for survival, for consciousness, for redemption. "Why should I have it so hard?" "Fuck it," the old reliable, lets me off the hook. When problems are ingested, when struggle occurs, we access our own natural order.

This is the paradox of existence: dying into life. Ego's house crumbles. Our Higher Self incarnates. We are no longer alone, unguided, unmirrored, unverified. A new consciousness comes to be—a visceral confirmation, a new awareness, an ally that stands side-by-side with us, that notices us, that accepts us from within. Suddenly we are seen. Then we see for the first time. Until we find the spiritual purpose of our lives, the strength to bring down the old order, the ego that has us imprisoned, the small self, we cannot live the natural path that occurs only when the ego dies. Then the Self-ego axis is restored. Ego lives but takes second position to a new sense of connection, awareness, and strength, a strength that comes from knowing that what your survival depended on died, but that you are now more alive than ever, a ravaged bride who has finally been impacted by life. Our fate is to be destroyed. Our destiny is to be strong enough to consciously participate in our own destruction. We need to experience this wound to earn access to our highest nature. God comes through the wound. God comes through experiencing death. Something needs to die so that we may live.

RICHARD FINDS HIS FIRE

"It haunts me. I see it over and over again. I am three years old, walking in Central Park with my mother, holding her hand. I am feeling secure in just being. It is late morning on a beautiful spring day, and the sun is just hovering above the treetops. We walk by the waterfall. I am enthralled by the sight and sound of water falling. I feel like sunshine itself. Suddenly seven or eight teenage boys abruptly descend from the top of the hill to the right of the waterfall. Their descent takes them right into our path. As they get near, my mother panics and completely lets go of me. She gropes for her pocketbook and throws it to them. Not a word has been spoken. No demand has been made. Whether my mother's interpretation of the situation was accurate is not the question. She felt threatened and saved herself. I no longer existed. Forsaken. Abandoned. Betrayed. From that day on I despised my mother and spent the next forty years trying to replace her with another, an adequate mother worthy of carrying the image of the Goddess. From that day on, I searched for this goddess in every other mother and woman that I saw. She would carry all my strength and adequacy. Redeem the mother. Redeem the Goddess. Redeem myself. This fantasy saved my life and then became my secret addiction."

All of Richard's conscious desire centered around his Goddess fantasy. Growing up, Richard's fight-and-fire would peek out only to return to his fantasy. Having lost the connection to his essence spirit, Richard lived an outer pretense. He pretended to be married, to own a business, to rescue his mother financially, to have children. But he was never really there. His heart and his energy secretly belonged to the craven image of his early fantasy. Everything was "as if."

There are two tricks we play in our initial survival: We forget the fire of our survival, and we become identified with the personality that we adopt. The wound or trauma secretly brings an experience of God. We separate this ecstatic life-saving experience from the pain that it solves.

Pain, disavowed, is compelled to be expressed. Pain holds our hidden fire. We must experience the wound consciously to reaccess our fire essence. Our Highest Nature brings us to this reenactment. We are programmed to lose everything. This was Richard's fate; he brings down the house with himself in it. Fire, wine, and war—Richard disavows these inner attributes, seeing these energies as outside himself, now envisioned in a fantasy woman worthy of this image.

Richard has taken the best in himself and given it away. Why must he do this? Because the secret is unbearable. What secret? For Richard the secret is: "It's all my fault. I am the cause. I must live the pain, for my mother, for the world." How to survive the pain and impulse for martyrdom? By acting out an all-encompassing fiery fantasy that holds our essential energy, a fantasy that reenacts our real desire, but outside ourselves. Why? Because the shame is so great that it is unbearable. Awareness takes ongoing struggle and the tension of opposites. Our war essence is needed to continue to be used for consciousness even when we achieve outer peace in our land. Inner war, outer peace. That's the equation. We stop fighting and became addicted to peace. No tension of opposites. No paradox. Only drunken arrogance and certainty. Our heroism brings us to this death-walk.

"There are no atheists in foxholes." In truth, only at the point of experiencing death do we make choices: Richard is guided to the point of death, and a part of him dies: the hero, the one who rescues his mother, the one who saves the business, the one who is more afraid of living than dying, the martyr. When our outer pain finally mirrors our true inner pain, then our truth can emerge. Richard stopped working at fixing; instead, he started feeling, remembering. He went back to his sunshine essence, the early one where he was sunshine itself. Going back in time he found his pain and expressed its truth viscerally, through feeling.

Jung, while concerned with the universal, was also concerned with the particular in human life. He devised a model of psychic structures and functions that all people shared in common and also explored how they came to be manifested in the unique combination that makes up the individual personality. These were known as "Psychological Types." While all people have the same psychological equipment to perceive what is happening outside and inside themselves and how to respond, each individual is different in his or her response. This is what is meant by a person's "type." The four types are "sensation," "thinking," "feeling," and "intuition." Each of us differs in our preference as to which of these types we use as our major mode of functioning.

Richard was the feeling type. Feeling tells you whether something is agreeable or not. When, as Richard did, you do this consistently, it gives rise to emotions but only when the feeling is powerful enough to trigger biochemical or neurological changes in the body. Its normal use is to make value judgment about inner or outer events to determine whether they are pleasant or unpleasant, beautiful or ugly. This requires reflection in the light of past experience.

Richard, as a feeling type, felt through his pain instead of disavowing it. When the pain itself is traveled through, your problem becomes the solution. Your real desire becomes embodied: The Self becomes manifest. Like peeling the layers of an onion, Richard got to his core, the sunshine self. And became it!

THE LEPER AND THE RAINMAKER: RETURNING TO YOUR ESSENCE

What is the nature of our nature? And, why is it important? Richard Wilhelm brought the story of The Chinese Rainmaker of Kiau Tchou to Jung. It parallels the figure of the Leper in the Old Testament. Both men, the Rainmaker and the Leper, are contaminated by the atmosphere in the city, by civilization. The prevailing collective—the people and the atmosphere of the city—are out of harmony with nature. There is unabated drought during the rainy season. Nothing can grow. A Rainmaker is brought to help.

Upon arriving, he immediately asks to be brought to a house at the edge of the city. He spends three days in the house alone; and when he emerges, it starts to snow. When Wilhelm asks him what he did to make that happen, he said,

> I come from another country where things are in order. Here they are out of order, they are not as they should be by ordinance of heaven. The whole country is not in Tao [flow of nature], and I am not in the natural order of things because I am in a disordered country. So I had to wait for three days until I was back in Tao, and then naturally the snow came.

There is a law that the Leper must stand outside the gates of the City for eight days. He is required to yell a warning for anyone who comes near, to stay away. The traditional understanding of this is that the leper is contaminated and he has the obligation to notify. He must protect the other. But in the story, exactly the opposite is true. The leper is there to return to his natural order. His task is to return to himself, to his essential order. It's the city's inhabitants that are contaminated. The leper's task is to return to his own nature. He needs to be aware and protect his return to essence from recontamination. When the Leper heals, the citizen inside the gates of the city is also restored to his/her own nature. When the Rainmaker reconnects to Tao, outer reality also changes. The weather, the whole atmosphere changes.

When the Leper reconnects to his "I," the whole city is redeemed. How many people does it take to reach the tipping point of change? Because of nonlocality, it manifests with one. A Hassidic story emphasizing this tells of a man praying on the holiest day of the year. To the Rabbi, it appeared as if the man was arguing with God. After the man stops praying, the Rabbi asked him what had happened: "I told God how angry I was for all the pain and misery that He allowed. But then I said, I guess if you can forgive me, I can forgive you." The Rabbi responded, "If you hadn't let God off the hook the messiah would be here." In other words, one man/woman's truth changes the world. The path to Self is through the truth of your individual experience. Not someone else's. Not through the collective. The reconnection to Self restores the Rainmaker, the Leper, and the whole community to its natural order.

Our spiritual struggle for individuation always occurs against collective opinions, demands, threats, and laws. The struggle itself affects everything within us and everyone around us. Because the gates of the city live inside us, we don't actually have to travel miles to decontaminate. We can create sacred space almost anywhere. The moment that we follow our experience and trust it, we are in sacred space, especially when all hell seems to be breaking loose, our imprinted nightmare seems to be unfolding, and we can't stop it. The gateways to the Self are within these disturbances.

Often the journey to the Self is initiated by a confrontation, a problem, a circumstance or person who threatens to ruin everything. A

Zen story about a student of Tea Ceremony illustrates this: In Feudal Japan, a young, peaceful Zen student is walking in the center of the village, when unexpectedly he steps on a glove that has fallen to the ground. Suddenly, the most famous Samurai in all Japan, and the greatest swordsman, confronts the young student and accuses him of stepping on the glove deliberately to make him lose face. Immediately, the Samurai challenges the young man to mortal combat and tells him to meet him at a designated spot just outside the city at sunrise. The Samurai promises that if the young man doesn't come he will find him and kill him. What to do?

This Samurai had earned a reputation for always keeping his word. The young man finds his Sensei, who tells him there is only one thing to do: "You must prepare to die. Go home, say prayers and put your affairs in order." As the young man was leaving, his teacher said: "Wait! Take this sword. Even though this is the greatest swordsman in all Japan, sometimes you can get lucky with the first thrust." The young man takes the sword, goes home and prepares to die. At sunrise, the young man with the sword finds the designated spot. He sits and waits. The Samurai comes, sees his fellow combatant and says, "I'm sorry, I made a mistake. I didn't realize you were a brother (meaning a brother Samurai warrior)."

Who organizes these confrontations? The center of the city symbolizes the Self. When the initiating action takes place from the center of the city, the Self is in charge. The Sensei is the young man's Higher Self guide. The Samurai is his Shadow, a disidentified aspect of the young man's nature that is demanding acceptance at this time. Nature is compelling wholeness of this being. Part of him is not enough. He is pushed by nature to be everything that he is, everything that he can be. To paraphrase Joe Louis, "You can run but you can't hide," from your own nature.

Jung distinguished between Self and the self of everyday, the ego. The goal of Self is the blueprint of humanity; it seeks this in the spirituality of art, religion, and the inner life of the soul. Jung felt that we can experience this as a profound mystery and as an expression of the God within.

While Jung was passionate in an affirmation of the Self as containing all the ingredients of a meaningful life, he was equally confirming of the shadow within us all. Though unwanted, in Jung's view, we take the shadow wherever we go as a dark companion. While we tend to ignore it, somehow it has its own way of intruding itself, particularly in our dream. Here, it appears as threatening, alien, hostile, leading to our feeling of distrust, anger, or fear. Jung, using the concept of archetypes, called this the Enemy or the Evil Stranger. Yet it is necessary for balance, and its coexistence can be seen in literature: Dorian Grey keeps his portrait hidden so that no one can see his evil secret life, and Dr. Jekyll and Mr. Hyde show the two sides of a single man, the healer and the evil one.

Jung suggests that to some extent we each have a "Dorian Grey" inside of us, a shadow to keep out of sight. To do this, we often project it onto others. Denying our own badness, attributing it to others, very often leads to a form of scapegoating and prejudice. Adolf Hitler, a prime example, was able to induce the German people to carry out his frightening programs, making the Holocaust possible. Contrarily, to own one's shadow is to become responsible so that ethical choices become possible. Shadow consciousness is thus critical to our well-being.

Returning to our last example, the Zen student was attached to beauty and peace. Lacking awareness, he was naïve. What was missing in the young man were warrior awareness and the courage of being prepared to die. Warrior awareness is a dedicated second level of consciousness, a more detached layer of impersonal awareness that notices. Without this awareness, we are unconscious lightning rods and victims to the fluctuations and storms of the moment. Feelings are facts; it's all personal. As slaves and robots, we have no free choice to say "no" or to stay and participate. It takes a warrior awareness—a fighting energy—to break the spell of our enslavement and martyrdom.

We parallel the Zen student in the sense that we develop and become invested in our adopted identity and personality and forget the initial fire and desire for life that triggered the behaviors that allowed us to survive. We become identified with these outer behaviors, identities, defenses, and compromises as if they were us. The initial fire, love and spirit behind these façades are consciously forgotten, but remain, secretly hidden in the plain sight of these outer behaviors.

Terms like *maladaptive* and *dysfunctional* are used to describe behaviors that are repetitive and problem-provoking. We must accept that the dream gate to the real desire, the soul's natural order and the individual's destiny, is through the manifested problem. Nature doesn't give us problems in order to change us but in order to return us to who we are. We dress and preserve our real desire in the clothing of behaviors that may look nothing like their hidden essence.

Jackie, a forty-three-year-old female shuts down and appears vegetative when confronted. Psychiatry has diagnosed her with Major Depression Recurrent. Accept that when you slow down her shut-down and connect to its movements, you notice that she shuts down aggressively, with a vengeance. So what looks like giving up and feeling hopeless turns out, in actuality, to be her warrior. Depression is her warrior. When the world sees her as withdrawn, scarred, it moves away in pity. The attention she gets and the punishment she secretly inflicts become a familiar repetitive dance, a secret gratification. Noticing only the overt problem behavior, Jackie's depression and acting overwhelmed, you miss the experience of the whole message. Overtly Jackie behaves weak and defeated. Inwardly, she's fighting mad and vengeful, the warrior in bloom.

When you slow it down you feel it. But first, you must trust that the problem contains the hidden story. The brief incongruity in Jackie's action reveals her life force and hidden higher nature. Without noticing, the drama of shut-down would be reenacted infinitely. Her essence would remain in shadow, projected onto others and lived vicariously in addictions and inappropriate relationships where her fighting essence would remain outside her identity.

Jung referred to this as ego development and the work of the first half of life. In the second half of life, the Self breaks through and the path of the Ego is joined to the Path of Wholeness. It is fated for our ego adaptation to be destroyed.

The ego stands to the self as the moved to the mover, or as object to subject. For Jung, reflecting on his own childhood experience, said that in childhood the ego can be identified with a number one personality and the Self with a number two. In this first half of life, the ego is needed to separate from parents, obtain a job or profession, marry and provide a home for the family. It is only in the second half of life that the ego recognizes its subordinate status to the Self, through the process of individuation. It is here that the ego begins to confront the Self and the Self the ego, all of which leads to the attainment of personality integration and higher consciousness.

Carl Jung, considered by many of his time to be both an eccentric and a unique individualist, was, most of all, the living embodiment of universal man. He came to realize his own human potential, deciding to live in an uncompromising way. His showed an uncanny understanding of what lies beneath the surface of our behaviors, and he kept faith with the truth as he saw it. He also cautioned, as we have suggested, that though such a life may include loneliness, it is the only path to follow. In the chapters to follow, we will continue to look ever more closely at Jung and his psychology to take full account of the life and personality of its founder, including looking at how we have included Jung's work, to our great joy, in our work. And remember: your problem *is* the solution.

CHAPTER 3

Shadow Figures as the Real You

The "shadow" contains all that is not accepted within us, both good and bad. For Jung, the personality we develop is a fragment of the totality of our nature. Jung called these splits "temporary solutions," provisional socialized adaptations that compel their diametric polar opposite to live in secrecy. We are the sum of these opposites.

Jung's idea is that the most satisfactory solution is a reintegration of the denied aspects of the Self, that opposites align in us to provide the opportunity for a new synthesis, greater than the sum of each individual fragment. This parallels religious and mystical sources, a return to our essence and the basis for the following chapter.

"I feel murder all around." A dark alley? A bad neighborhood? No. Just a typical social situation where Bill, a shy, fifty-four year-old male, has reverted to his familiar "outsider" role in a social environment. The politeness feels murderous, the atmosphere annihilating. A life-long ghost, Bill finds himself pulling back and hiding. Physically, he withdraws to a point of invisibility. Simultaneously, he also notices an ever-present rage that he hides. The rage is so automatic, familiar, and repetitive, that Bill hardly notices it anymore. He says that what always happens as an "outsider" is that he feels a pervasive judgment of the others as stupid, shallow, selfish, and arrogant. Asked to sense into the atmosphere that is coming at him, Bill says, "it's very aggressive." Staying awake with the experience of the aggressive atmosphere, Bill looks up in revelation and says: "I feel murder all around."

Bill's posture is slumped forward while also receding back, and he is encouraged to follow his forward slump with head leaning forward, and go further into it. Slumping forward seems to be falling forward to the floor, but leaning back at the same time nullifies this imbalance. As he goes farther into his bend, he is asked what he feels. He says, "It's like the coil of a snake, waiting to pounce. This feels normal, coiling, ready to pounce. I'm no longer scared. The gist of it is that these murderers don't have anything on me."

Going further, the therapist has Bill imagine a figure that contains this energy. Trusting the energy of the coil, Bill goes deeper and, at a certain point, springs up. His face is now awake, involved, and present. Bill is transformed, and a warrior emerges. This warrior makes no apologies, feels no envy of the murderous others and no self-pity. The warrior is awake, alert, and aware, contained and leaning forward. Knowing the murderer in yourself makes you whole.

Do you ever feel yourself overwhelmed by a powerful emotion over which you have no control, one which you do not know where it came from? Do you trust the importance of your experience or do you join with your rational mind that dismisses the disturbance and criticizes yourself for your inadequacy and distractibility? Notice how Bill's body and repetitive social reaction actually holds the essence of his participation. What are these shadow figures/players that engage and combine to form Bill's "warrior" essence?

First: we have the collective: polite, civilized but secretly murderous. Their socially acceptable expression engenders fear due to anger, rage, and the aggressive intent that lies underneath an overt behavior that follows the rules of society, the consensual reality of the group.

Second: the secret snake in you, ready to coil and strike. Take Bill: every time he resumes his position as an outsider, the muscles in his gut, the tension in his spine show. The very murderous aspect he sees in others, is revealed in himself.

Third: the fearful hider: Our most recurring secret is that we are the desperate, helpless, vulnerable, alone, and unacceptable little person of our first trauma.

Of these three shadows, "the fearful hider" is the closest to Bill's conscious, familiar, and primary identity and represents the realm of personal shadow and the rational mind. The murderer and the snake are collective unconscious shadow figures, archetypal forces experienced outside the Self. Why does an essence decompose into separate streams? It's our thermostat. This goes to the paradox of nature, not that something is created from nothing, but that nothing was created from something. That "something" that has always existed is "essence." Essence exists first, then comes darkness. Darkness births revelation. To Jung, the spark of our life comes from the darkest spot. He saw the light, the fire of desire that darkness holds. Our lack, our deficit, our diminishment holds the fire of our life-force and all meaning.

For totality, we have to go backward in time to the essence, not forward. Ongoing relativity and tension between our known diminished reality and our essence level always exists. We know when we are not home, even though there is a pretense that we are home, that we are ourselves. Our essence needs a vessel and a mirror. Our desire is the vessel. A detached awareness creates the Center for the mirror.

Wholeness is imprinted from inception. We are wholeness waiting for a place to happen. And we attempt its realization regardless of whether or not there is a vessel to receive it. Instinct takes us right there. We see the other, we expect a vessel, to receive our light and to share it in return. Like instincts that awaken in an animal in response to outer stimuli, our own vessel and our own conscious self-reflection and verification depend on an initial shared experience of reflection with another. When that does not occur, essence fragments.

To redeem wholeness, we go backward to the essence, not forward, retrieving each fragment along the way. What drives us to do this? Ongoing tension. Our essence level always exists. We know when we're not home. But there is a pretense that we are, that we are not ourselves. The initial attempt to actualize our wholeness leaves us wanting.

THE PROCESS IS LOSS, AND LOSS IS
THE SEED OF REAL DESIRE

All revelation in our physical and dreaming worlds brings an inferior or partial polarization of the essence. By the time we give words or form to a great insight, or actualize an inspiration, it's a turd, a distorted shell of the high dream. Our ability to track our own process parallels the observation of sub-atomic particles. An electron can only be observed at the point where a reflection occurs, where it hits the electron counter. A collapsing principle is always necessary. All manifestation requires this reflection. We do not see directly; we only see and know what we ourselves can reflect and mirror. A reflecting retina is required. Bringing an image or dream to awakened reality occurs in an awakened state where both realities are perfect mirror images of each other. We create the reality we mirror.

Being stuck in a polarity and only identified with one of the poles will evoke its exact mirror image outside. Bring an attachment to a passive pole with a secret aggressive pole in the background, and the world will be compelled to bring its mirror of your disavowed aggression right at you. When your own aggression lurks secretly in the background, it's like lightning looking for circuitry. Because each pole is a hologram of the other, each pole an imprint of the other. That is why there is always an essential oneness between the most disparate opposites awaiting reexperience and conscious inclusion. In this way, we unconsciously bring our most disavowed, threatening natures right to our door. And each person on the planet is a hologram of everything in the universe ready to mirror your disavowed nightmare. Be careful what you disavow, because your secret nature flirts with the entire universe to find its reflection.

With or without awareness, lightning strikes. Are we under attack, or being guided? Do we connect to the disturbing as a possibility, a doorway to a stream of our nature striving to join the river of our wholeness? Unaware, we're the victim. In awareness, we're guided. The images we see, the sensory grounded experiences and thoughts we have, are reflections similar to the moment of observation when an electron hits a counter. We do not know the path of an electron or the bigger dream or the intention behind its path. We only notice the electron and its quality from its one fixed point of observation. Until then it's a wave, a subtle experience or tendency at the periphery of our awareness, without form. At the point of collision, it transforms to a particle observed and noticed in conventional reality.

Our rational mind operates like an electron counter and remains in the certainty that what you see is all there is. Familiar, reflected images and experiences do not threaten. Those images and experiences alien to us and out of our sense of control disturb. Disavowed, these images and energies are scary and problematic. Split from the essence level, they appear big and overwhelming. Ironically, these big, victimizing energies and experiences are the dream gate entrance to the larger experience. How paradoxical that the entry requires joining or wrestling the very energy that may destroy us. A spiritual heroism and warriorness is required to stay engaged. In climbing the staircase to the Self essence, wrestling these shadows are the steps that get you there. The entry point of each wrestle is the disturbing problem.

WHY A NEED TO DREAM?

Why dream about what literally happened during the day? Why would we need this recapitulation? Weren't we there the first time? Probably not. Because the first time we were not there, no deep reflection occurred. No participation. No impact. Why pray aloud? Who is listening? Are you listening? By actually listening, are you consciously awakening? Is anyone listening when you're not? Praying to God only outside yourself, are you asleep? Imagine being stuck in longing for connection and relationship and seeking it outside yourself in a person, image, or God that is the answer. There is the inevitable repetitive rejection or seduction that actually occurs when you approach someone with no internal connection in yourself. Your shadow rejecter will find a perfect mirror in outer reality and actualize you and your others pulled by compulsion to repeat this transaction until your own rejecter comes to light. When what you seek is outside the self, you bring your dismissed "you" and actualize it. Here's the big secret: It takes a relationship within yourself to realize a relationship outside yourself. By listening, hearing, and being impacted, can you imagine what you may synchronize with others?

The shadow rejecter contains all that we reject within ourselves: our self-rejection expert. Unconscious, it runs rampant, despising ourselves and others, unrelentingly critical and perfectionistic. But, what is the true nature and intent of this negative energy? What does a "rejecter" look like before it becomes so big that it's an unconscious shadow operating outside the periphery of our identity? Can you imagine the "No!" and free choice–permission essence at the heart of this energy? It is the "No" that bestows definition, boundaries, permission, and desire. Permission to make a life, the right to choose and not be victimized, the power to take, to receive, to give out of love rather than obligation or survival? Can you imagine how valuable and necessary this capacity secretly is? How this essence breaks the spell of compulsion, fate, and victimization? How our seemingly negative and most dangerous shadow figure energies hold the Self?

Jim says: "I fail at everything I try." He's been saying it for twenty-five years. Has he never heard it? Until Jim actually hears his own words, this dream, "I fail at everything I try," remains a free-floating ghost in the background of his life. Hearing the words brings the dream into existence. When he feels it viscerally, deep in his gut, "I fail at everything I try" becomes the point of reflection and awareness where he enters the dream. Only when Jim hears his own words is there somebody home within him to notice and reflect. When he hears his own words, he wakes up. The image at the dream-gate looks like failure, but by entering the stream, we never know where the river will take us. We can only trust that its very flow is our nature and that by steeping ourselves in it we join what's pushing to happen.

What was really going on with Jim? When he disavowed his heart's agenda, the biggest part of him refused to go along. Jim's rational decisions did not include the heart. For example, when Jim re-created his failure atmosphere and leaned into its direction, trusting that it had a purpose, it was then that he felt the warmth of his missing heart respond. He knew. He said, "My heart has been missing from all my ambitions." Finding that each experience we have has a linear direction congruent with each energy or experience we know may be new to some, but this idea has been used since ancient times by shamans, prophets, and prayers to amplify an experience through the body. Once you identify the energy, you bring the body into it. In the East, one can't even imagine any experience that excludes the body. Jim repeated, "I fail at everything I try." Making a gesture that exemplifies his statement, he pointed his right forefinger in accusation. Experimenting by repeating his gesture even more emphatically, he smiled and concurred that "accusation" was the energy. Jim's ongoing ghostly atmosphere is "accusation." Further experimenting by taking steps in many directions, Jim found that southeast was the direction of "accusation." Walking slowly and then leaning southeast, the realization struck. "My heart has been missing from all my ambitions."

Jim's heart energy restored, his priorities changed from who he was supposed to be to who he really is, Jim can now complete the dream. Success for Jim requires being heart-full. John F. Kennedy said, "Success has a thousand fathers, failure is an orphan." Jim's heart essence is the dance between failure and success. Why not just go for success? Because "success" is only one side of a polarity. Being attached to the pole of success may be very attractive and glorifying. But it ensures that the other side must be expressed.

FAMILY POLARITY

How often do you see two brothers or sisters caught in this polarity, one sibling successful and the other a "black sheep?" We'd like to see the day when the successful sibling thanks the failing sibling for occupying that role: "Dear brother, I want to thank you for being such a great screw-up, freeing me to be golden and take all that life has to offer. After all, I had about as much conscious choice falling into my role as you did in yours. I could never be as good a failure as you, even if I tried. If I've neglected you, I'm sorry. Don't forget, we only measure ourselves by those above us and not the ones below. Even in the moments when I noticed your suffering, it was better you than me. I appreciate the opportunity you gave me. Now it's your turn."

Getting stuck primarily in one pole of a polarity is our fate. Then, the other pole, the less familiar aspect, often attributed to others secretly envied or despised, becomes problematic and symptomatic. And what's trying to happen is the interaction and integration of both poles, not just the one that looks superior. Our fate is to be stuck in an unresolved polarity. Our destiny is to go back to our essence by reexperiencing the dance and oneness between our poles. Our problems bring the missing pole. With two disparate poles and our detached awareness, the three forces of our own circuitry are in place. Our inner trinity, our two poles and our higher awareness, which can hold the tension of opposites, reconnects us consciously to our infinite source, which Jung called the Self.

Nadine, a forty-two-year-old woman, starts the conversation with a confession: "Just before I came, I ate a lot of chocolate, devoured three pieces of gooey cake, and then ate out." She blurts this out in a split second. Are her eating and confession in sync? At times, she acts totally dependent, as if her very existence hinges on myself and others. The confession and the dependence disturb because they are incongruent double messages; the overt words of the confession express guilt, remorse, and realization, but Nadine also expresses an aggressive suddenness, manipulation, and enjoyment at getting away with it.

Overtly, Nadine acts dependent, as if she is fragile, eternally needs your help and guidance, but her implication is threatening, as if something horrible will happen to you or her if you don't comply with being there to rescue her.

Nadine dreams that two woman are robbing her. The two female robbers symbolize a shadow thief coming into consciousness. Maybe you can also sense this thief in the "aggressive-suddenness-manipulation-and-enjoyment-of-getting-away-with-it" part of her confession. The coinciding dream is a confirmation.

Diagnostically, medicine has been happy to bestow a diagnosis of eating disorder, bulimia, bipolar disorder, or borderline personality. And Nadine does not identify as a thief or want to be called one. What essence could the thief carry? Using the eating, bingeing behavior as a way of entering the dream, Nadine demonstrates how she grabs chocolate, suddenly and without restriction. She grabs the chocolate so quickly, furiously, and suddenly that she completely overwhelms any possible resistance. She grabs and grabs using both hands. Slowing down the grabbing movements but keeping their intensity, Nadine's energy seems to spread, from a locus in her hands and arms to her whole body. She grows right before your eyes: "I'm big. I'm strong. I know exactly what to do."

As she starts to demonstrate her strength, she suddenly sits down, gives up, and says: "I'm nauseous." As she reverts to being weak and helpless, the nausea gets worse: "I don't want to be strong, I need you to be strong for me." Nadine says, "I'm scared to be strong. It's too hard and not safe. I don't want to do it!" As soon as something is said, Nadine responds angrily, "Don't tell me what to do." She is strong. She is clear. She is big. And she is self-dependent.

In this encounter, one can actually feel being dreamt up to say or do something wrong so that the other can be angry, strong, and OK by herself. Suddenly, it's Nadine who is strong, clear, and self-determined.

Then the edge: sudden fear. Self-criticism. The perceived danger of revealing her strength openly. "You're bad," her critic says, "selfish. How dare you take for yourself without giving to the other first? You are nothing." Or even worse, "you're killing me. I can't take it." As Nadine repeats what her critic is saying, nausea overtakes her. She slumps and gives up.

Say something at this perfect time and the cycle restarts. "Don't tell me what to do!" Follow the anger, the determination, the clarity, the "No." Big Nadine is back. Both the thief and the stealthy relationship interaction support a Big Nadine, clear, strong, direct, and independent. But without awareness, this resumes in cyclical repetitive drama with the high dream essence of independent strength remaining outside Nadine's identity. A dangerous strength that appears as a thief.

Every time Nadine gives up, she ultimately pounces. She gets Big. She gets clear. For Nadine to sustain her Bigness she must stay conscious and present. She relates her Bigness to a song. It has its own beat and rhythm, its own awareness. Nadine asks the question, "What should I do now?" Instead of answering and recapitulating the cycle, Nadine now reestablishes the posture, gesture, and movement of Big Nadine. She stands with strength and bigness, and from that posture and Big essence, Big Nadine answers the small one in her who asks, "What should I do now?" Big Nadine responds, "I need to be here with you all the time."

What does it mean to be here with you? Nadine experimented and then demonstrated. She comes behind and physically supports the shoulders and guides them. She shows exactly how it feels. It feels good and strong, not alone for the first time. And then we switch. And she is guided, and she feels perfect—not alone, no compulsion, just peaceful. And the visceral experience of not being alone, of being OK, and of being totally present restores. Consciousness takes two. For a minute, an hour, a day, a lifetime, the essence incarnates. Will she repeat the cycle? The familiar repetition? Will she live her essence consciously or let it drive her unaware from the background?

Have you ever had someone who seemingly invites care, asks for advice, and then attacks you for it? To bite the hand that feeds seems to be the pathology of our times. Strange as it may seem, beneath this pathology is an essence of independence, self-determination, and permission to receive. Nadine demonstrates how dependence, entitlement, and stealth, so abhorrent to the observer, actually hold her biggest strength. Will Nadine go back to the existential familiar or continue her journey?

Ben, a fifty-one-year-old male, complains of a chronic, low-grade depression he has suffered since adolescence. This is his dream: "I'm a counselor at a sleep-away camp. My job is to coach and organize the basketball activities for the kids. But there is no basketball. A little boy around seven has taken it and won't tell where he hid it. My job is to speak to this little boy and convince him to return the ball. I feel powerless over this little boy and sense that he will reject anything that I say. But I start to speak to him anyway. To my surprise, he responds to me and, taking me by the hand, leads me to the missing basketball, which he has hidden in plain sight."

Let us remember what the original problem is: chronic depression. From the fifty-one-year-old perspective, energy, joy and connection are missing. Why? Because the dream reveals that there is a seven-year-old Ben, isolated, not known, and not talked to. Stuck in that position, Little Ben is invisible, angry, and depressed. Symbolizing the Self, the basketball is in his sole possession. And it's hidden. The Self is our source of all life and vitality. Hidden, we are cut off, lifeless, faking it all the way. What is the relevance of the dream? That when Big Ben related to Little Ben, the flow of Ben's life-force resumes; his true soul, carried by the image of the boy, is now accepted and he is whole as he had never been. This wholeness now requires the conscious relating of Big Ben to Little Ben. What does that mean in our world? The way we feel and the problems we have are often attributed to being stuck in childhood.

The problem, however, is not the child. It's spitting out a big adult. The child has been there for a long time. It's Big Ben that needs rebirth. Without this bigness, we're fated to be orphans. In all of this, where is your shadow? Where do you find it? Don't look too far. Number one can be found in the people you hate, the second in the people you want to avoid, the third in the people you admire or look up to. Since everyone you dream is you, everyone who appears in your dream is a potential shadow, seeking light. They all carry an important message and viewpoint. In fact, an excellent method for understanding your dream is to become each of the figures in your dream and act them out until you get the truth of their message, energy, and mindset. This especially includes the people you hate, the people you avoid, the people you love, and the people you're meeting for the first time. Animals, places, and objects in the dream are also to be related to.

The dream continues day and night. Enlightenment requires that we enter the dream to grow. By entering the dream lucidly, we take the images, feelings, and messages evoked and relate them to what's going on in our everyday world. Dreams are compensatory. In other words, they are sent to you to alert you to what needs your attention. So, dreams mirror what's going on internally. Since internal and external are synchronized, your internal reality creating the outer, the dream then reveals the thread between your inner and outer events. This gives you the choice to consciously join what nature is trying to unfold.

Diane, a successful real estate manager, broker, and developer, complains of difficulty making and carrying out decisions. Coinciding with her complaint, Diane must evict a very difficult tenant whom she fears. Encouraged to just walk her regular walk and pay attention to any contradictory tendency that arises, Diane notices a subtle tendency for her left foot to get stuck in the ground and make her trip. It's as if the foot wants to stay right there. Repeating the walk to the point where she feels this "staying," she is encouraged to get to the place where the foot wants to stay and actually "stay." Diane walks and suddenly stops. Her feet are now firmly planted. "They don't want to move." Her head tilting slightly forward it is suggested that she follow the tilt of her head, going forward with what the head is already doing. Diane responds positively to the recommendation. Bringing out this initial head tilt tendency, Diane bends farther forward amplifying its direction.

Leaning farther forward, Diane suddenly looks up in realization. Her busy mind has stopped. Her legs firmly planted, suddenly she finds herself focused and certain. "I refuse to budge." As she stands there, head bent over, her feet firmly planted, she is asked: "What figure does this remind you of?" It reminded her of a bull. Being Big for Diane looks like a bull. Diane is physically petite, but when she is in her full bull-energy body, she is a large presence.

The next day Diane confronted the tenant directly, refusing to take "no" for an answer. Once she made her decision, she planted her feet, put her head down, and pushed through. She did not let her rational mind, tenant's trickery, or falling into pity maneuver her into giving in. She refused. The tenant was gone in forty-eight hours.

This experience exemplifies how a process that is trying to happen is always right there. Any problem that finds you flirts with your biggest nature. Also, we have preconceived ideas about what the Center looks like. For Diane, her Higher-Self looks like a bull. She may think it was supposed to be some highly evolved, brilliant being, but her momentary Center, the one that brings completion, is her bull. There is no escape. Shadow always seeks reflection and inclusion. The flirts persist.

A new psychologist begins working in a drug rehab. It doesn't take long before her idealism about impacting her clients takes quite a hit. As she comes to know her clients better, she finds herself envying the heroin addicts: "Here I am responsible and worried about my every action. These people do whatever they want, get away with it, and suffer no consequences." That night she dreams: "I secretly use ten bags of heroin every day." Taking the dream seriously, she stopped pretending that she did not operate with the same ruthless trickery and for the self alone, manipulating her clients. Initially, she felt caught, exposed. Then she began accepting this in herself, seeing her own self-serving agendas and ruthless manipulations. It takes one to know one! More than that, it takes one to treat one. Internally, it takes one to realize one. Once she knew this in herself and accepted her shadow, her capacity to relate and interact with her clients became natural. And her right to express her own real desire openly and honestly came with it. To date, the absurdity of identifying with her secret agenda has been her greatest insight. Such a nice girl. Such a selfish agenda. So proud of it.

Though universal, the shadow, our disowned personality, is an individual and subjective experience. Shadow is in the eyes of each beholder, influenced by family, culture, atmosphere, and mores. The same family members have different shadows and can be each other's shadow. In fact, within family, group, and society, there is a distribution of shadow in roles, strata, class, and hierarchy. Subjectively, each individual's own experience, noticed and taken seriously, is the path to the Self. The subjective, personal experience is a royal road to enlightenment as old as time but marginalized by the collective culture and rational mindset of civilization.

Marginalizing our most intense and subtle experiences as delusions, distractions, and fantasies, thus shutting off our deepest awareness, nature, and dream, invites chaos, symptoms, and destruction by what we disavow. The real you notices. The real you accepts these experiences: noticing, witnessing, and joining them to know their energy. Behind your nature are deep structured forms awaiting release and actualization. Dependent on environmental stimuli, response, and mirroring for realization, archetypes organize as complexes where the essence nature and vitality stay unconscious. What becomes manifest is a distorted, and polarized, split-off form of essence hardly resembling our imprinted archetypal endowment.

Frank, thirty-five, complains, "Everyone thinks I'm weird. When I go up to a girl I feel her say, 'What's wrong with you?' I feel this criticism all the time. It gets me down." Frank says, "the criticism that there is something wrong with me is there all the time." Frank's problem is that he enters every task, meeting, and challenge, feeling internally criticized. Frank demonstrates a gesture and facial expression that captures the criticism "What's wrong with you?" He makes a face, eyes out of contact, and looks down in disinterest. Going further, looking down, and no longer even pretending to be in contact, Frank smiles and says, "Feels good. I choose No. But I can also choose Yes." Now Frank has spent most of his conscious life satisfying his mother, honoring obligations to his family, subjugated to his sense of correctness in social actions. He has not followed or identified his own desire because his permission/endowment to choose, to say "yes" or "no" in line with his own needs or heart-full passion did not exist. This vital feminine essence, Frank's own Holy Grail permission "for thee" realization was retrieved by wrestling the negative critic that brought him down. This is nothing short of Frank's right to be in the world on his own behalf, to engage, not hide, his heart, to experiment with love, and to choose. Stay or leave? Yes or No. Can you see how the problem complex holds the essence Choice, and how Choice would instinctually arise at the point of any engagement? The problem holds the solution "Choice" to Frank's repetitive spell. Thus, with You as permission, you rejoin the search for the Self.

CHAPTER 4

God as Shadow

"Religion is a defense against the experience of God."

—Carl Jung

Once upon a time God was everywhere. Like the certainty of the sun rising, He/She could be seen, felt, and experienced. All of nature was a constant witness and partner to our own awareness. Jung used the term "participation mystique" to describe a oneness and a universal soul that exists between all things, animate and inanimate.

Mortal man's visceral experience of God was embodied in the female goddesses such as Aphrodite, Sophia, Venus, Demeter, Persephone. In the era of the First Temple (961 BC to 568 BC) the Shekinah, this female aspect of God, was omnipresent. God wasn't an intellectual idea: He/She was a feeling experience. People saw energy. People knew love. People felt awe. People naturally dreamt into the essence of the other and into the soul of matter. All was open for all to see and feel into. Experience didn't stop at the physical boundary. Everything was alive. What went wrong?

They saw God only as the other and outside themselves. Because they projected their reality onto others, they took no responsibility for it. Their circumstance and environment were God's providence. Not theirs. They took no responsibility to be co-creators and made no connection to the impact of their behavior or intentions on the world they lived in. Becoming proficient at objectifying the raw forces of nature outside themselves, they cleaved to graven images rather than knowing and harnessing these forces in themselves, to be all they could be, to find the path of their nature and their soul's calling. As civilization advanced, the visceral experience of God became hidden.

Initially, the remnant of the experience of God remained in His/Her laws, rituals, and the spirit behind them. Soon, only the Law remained. The Rational Mind, which creates order, structure, and control, became King.

A German myth that reflects this says Aphrodite has been living in a cave in Bavaria for two thousand years. The feminine remains in Shadow. The experience of God, the passion of the heart, lives in a cave. Not just in Germany, but in us. There is no bride. No inner-other. We pretend to belong, but we feel alone in the midst of our fellow orphans. Until the problem, the malady, the wound that won't be ignored. That is, until the pain is so great, the suffering so intense that the pretense of control, certainty, and belonging can no longer be sustained. That is Job's story.

ENTER THE SHADOW: YOUR BIG "I" KNOCKS AT YOUR DOOR

The ongoing theme that appears throughout the Judeo/Christian tradition is a provocative Satan figure making a bet with God to prove man/woman unworthy. This bet is behind the would-be sacrifice of Isaac at the hands of his father, Abraham; the sufferings of God's righteous servant Job; and the earthly temptations flung at a mortal Christ. We need this bet to access our deepest reality: that we are not passive participants but co-creators with God. Our mortal selves want no part of this challenge because to do so means taking on risk, assuming responsibility, and, most terrifying, going into the unknown.

When Peter (Of Little Faith) reached for Jesus and walked on water, he acceded to this higher reality. Images like walking on water and burning bushes that are not consumed by the fire reflect a state of being in two realities at the same time.

Remember Adam's sin? The "sin" wasn't that Adam ate from the Tree of Knowledge. It's that he ate only from the Tree of Knowledge. He had completely disconnected from the Tree of Life. Even in the Garden of Eden, Adam was confronted by his own rational mindset, as if his choice was either one or the other and that he could only connect to one reality at a time, when in fact, he was perfectly endowed to be in two realities simultaneously. That was his essence, as it is ours, and it was disavowed instantly. Upon eating from the Tree of Knowledge, Adam became completely consumed by his physical experience, as if no other reality existed. The rational mind eliminates anything it doesn't sense. This is being drunk in one reality. Consciousness, awareness, and here-and-nowness require being awake to the tension of two simultaneous realities. When we are able to hold this tension, awakened, we can follow the process and revelation that is unfolding before us. And we can participate. We can choose: "yes" or "no."

ABRAHAM'S CHOICE

When Abraham was confronted by God's order to sacrifice his son, Isaac, he could have used a lawyer's trick to get out of it by holding God to his previous covenant—that Abraham and Isaac would be the fathers of a great nation. But Abraham's essence, his Higher Self, was here to fix the world. He chose to participate in what was unfolding before him. By proceeding to enact God's commandment to sacrifice Isaac, Abraham incurred an eternal debt. God owed him one! And He/She liked it. This eternal debt would extend to all mankind. Abraham uses his Shadow consciously to manipulate a better world by harnessing his darkest, earthly nature for its spiritual purpose. At the very moment of Isaac's binding, the world changed.

Was God really tricked or was Abraham a perfect mirror for the highest intention? Does God need a mirror or Abraham's reflection of Him/Herself? Does Abraham need his own reflection? Yes. The deepest nature of nature, everything in the universe, participates in reflecting on itself, seeing itself, bringing itself to consciousness. Symbolically, the action of Isaac's sacrificial binding represents a conscious restriction of our inborn desire to receive merely for the self alone. This endows human beings with the possibility of being emancipated from acting out their base appetites and limited reality. Is this not a contradiction? To bind a son, conceived late in life, for death sacrifice? No. Because Isaac represents a part of Abraham and therefore the part of us that is our unrestricted pure desire; Abraham and Isaac are two separate worlds, two separate realities in each of us.

Abraham embodies the world to come, our highest spiritual nature and love. Isaac embodies our here-and-now mortal consciousness, close to our animal nature and appetites. The actual binding must come by choice. Abraham chose to bind Isaac. Isaac, at age thirty-seven, chose to participate. Why? Because it was his turn to use his true nature in the service of his soul. By submitting, Isaac experienced a form of death not unlike that of Jesus' death on the cross. What died was the part of himself that thought he was the center of the universe, the self-absorbed "me." Both Jesus and Isaac felt forsaken at the moment of mortal death. They personify dying into life, our higher nature to transcend to a new realm and greater reality. Isaac's greater reality, his Big "I," is called Awe. God comes through the wound. Isaac and his emerging blindness symbolize going inside, operating and knowing from within, from genuine feeling, from mortal acceptance, from being a conscious vessel.

JOB AND THE COSMIC BET

Because it is imprinted in us, the bet and its imperative won't be denied. This motif appears cross-culturally in myths, plays, stories, and rituals throughout humanity; God playing dice with humans. How do we know that Shadow is the point of action where God directly participates? That was the healing revelation in the Book of Job. The story says that God appeared to Job in a whirlwind, in a storm. As the experience unfolded, God became the Behemoth and the Leviathan. "Behold the Leviathan which I made as I made you." The Behemoth is the animal monster who rules the animal world. The Leviathan is the sea monster who rules that world. The latter is known as an aspect of Satan, the Devil. There is an understanding that every word in the Bible is a name of God. Satan is a name of God. Snake is a name of God. Curses is a name of God. Job sees God in all his forms and realizes that at any moment the Center, the place of God and Self, exists when these disturbing shadow forces present themselves. Change is about to happen. This truth breaks the trance of civilized naïveté, that nature can be reduced to rational understanding, dialogue, control, and law. "Love thy neighbor as thyself." Superficially, love the other. Go deeper, and the other is you. Deeper still, the neighbor is God. Even deeper, adding your neighbor to you, you become your Big "I." Deeper yet, your "I" is the aggregate of all your Big "I's." Deepest of all, your "I" is your Individuation path, the path of your destiny.

In physics, a beam of light and its direction is the sum of all the photon vectors that go into it. In every beam, you can observe a "tail," the discernable shadow behind the beam that determines its path and direction. Like a beam of light, our direction is also determined by our tail, our shadow. Alcohol is recovery's tail. Disavow alcohol, move on to the new by putting the alcohol behind you, you stay stuck there. Instead, you must build on it, know it in you, and accept it. Then you can transcend back to your essence. You become your Big "I."

Alcohol is the tail that supports the beam of light, the "I." Like the tail of the spine supporting kundalini, the snakelike life energy that rises from the tail of the spine to higher chakras in the heart, then the head, then above the head, you start at the tail; the tail supports everything. What is the Big "I" of alcohol? It's the initial spontaneous archetypal energy and experience that the alcohol brought. It's going back to that wonderful, instant, whole-making experience that this shadow completes when embraced. Disavowed, or secretly stored in a complex of behaviors, beliefs, and repetitions that see the alcohol as outside oneself, we remain fixated, compulsively driven by the alcohol's disavowed energy. Why does alcohol have to do with religion? Jung understood the desire for alcohol as a desire for God; he believed that alcohol brings a visceral experience of God. Jung said, "Religion is a defense against the experience of God." When alcohol brings this experience, the resulting compulsion and repetitive, ritualized behavior that we call addiction parallels religion, law, and tradition that refers to, but never joins, the initial experience of God.

Matthew's Gospel traces the lineage of Jesus. Superficially, this is used as historical, genetic evidence that Jesus was the messianic inheritor. But what this really means is that Jesus is an accumulation of Big "I's." Abraham, Isaac, Jacob, Joseph, Elijah. The messianic process is in us as Individuation.

The first commandment says, "I am the Lord your God." This means that when God shows up in the shadow forms that Job witnessed, that's where the action is. That's where God is. We are animated by our problems and disturbances because they are the source of our Individuation. We are compelled to be all the "I" we can be. The action, process, or Tao of our age is in the "I," not in looking for God outside ourselves. Our consciousness and participation creates the field where our shadow polarities, our separated dualistic worlds, are re-engaged. The oneness between these seeming opposites retrieves our "I" essence from shadow.

PERMISSION TO HAVE AN "I"

The Parsifal myth of finding the Holy Grail symbolizes earning this realization. A young knight of the Round Table in King Arthur's Court, Parsifal, sets out to find the Holy Grail, Jesus' magical chalice. Parsifal enters the Kingdom of the Fisher King adorned in a remnant of his mother's garment. The wounded king spends all of his time fishing (going into the unknown) to find relief from the pain of his wound, usually depicted as a wound to the mouth suffered as a young man who caught a golden magical fish that burned his mouth when he tried to eat it.

Unknown to Parsifal, the castle of the Fisher King is also the Castle of the Holy Grail, where every night there is a procession where the Chalice is displayed. The king is so consumed by his wound that he doesn't realize that the healing and restoring Chalice is in his very own house. Many years later an older, withered Parsifal returns to the Kingdom. This time he hears the procession and the words "Whom does the Grail serve?" When Parsifal answers "It serves thee," the king is restored, the wound is healed, and the redeemed king rules for three days (symbolically a full, dynamic sequence) and dies.

Isaac, Job, and the Fisher King are metaphors for God coming through the wound, through the problem. You experience God by trusting your experience and following it. We seem to be required to die into life to break through the trance, certainty, and rational mindset of our time and reexperience the natural flow of our feelings, energy, heart, and desire that is ours. The feminine restores us to our unique path and individuation.

One way to view the Chalice is to see it as the Feminine, the fourth element that completes the trinity. The healing realization is that this world is created for us to receive, for us to live our true "I" nature and that this realization must be retrieved from shadow. Our Big "I" knows this, but as wounded kings, queens, and mother-bound knights, (symbolized by Parsifal's attachment to his mother's garment), we are all alone. Without the true Feminine, without feeling and Eros, there is no acceptance or room for the new, no permission for an "I." Instead, we have the extreme dichotomy of martyrdom/victimization at one pole and unfettered greed, aggression, and entitlement at the other. Neither pattern chooses life, love, or accesses real desire, the path of the heart, awakened and feeling, in the here-and-now.

Dylan, eleven, gets very excited and thinks he can fly. He has just had his third, severe injury from bounding into the air from a high place, without regard for gravity. He's made three visits to the emergency room recently and had three broken bones. The psychiatrists are calling this mania and bipolar disorder. Dylan doesn't seem to have any problem flying, it's the falling and hitting the ground that throws him. In his mind, he's a "flier," not a "faller." His metaphor for what's trying to happen is in the falling: that's where the action is. Something in the falling, in the landing, is exactly what Dylan needs to be whole. How do we know? Because the falling and the resulting pain keeps happening. The rational intervention is, for Dylan, to experience the consequences of his actions. How dare he be so ecstatic that he thinks he can fly? The consensus reality will see this ecstasy as dangerous, life threatening, and destructive. This process, for Dylan, is learning how to fall, feeling the ground. He is the sum of flying and falling, a magical third that includes both.

Falling is the momentary Center for Dylan. It is the point of action. How does one know? Because God resides in the action that keeps happening beyond our conscious intent. It's up to us to synchronize what's happening right before our eyes with nature's intent. That's the Eastern concept of Tao. That's the idea of the Center: to realize that, at any moment, in time, God's intent takes the form for what's trying to happen to make us whole. Dylan's shadow is the falling, feeling the ground, his mortality. His confrontation with his shadow brings wholeness: spending an hour falling and landing feeds him laughter and enjoyment. Repetition and compulsion always brings us to the point of our essence, if we are conscious. And metaphors, symbols, and representations are then synchronized with every part of us and every part of the universe. If you can experience the natural order, Tao, even in one finger, you can bring it to everything. And, if you're in Tao, the whole world is healed.

This process of wholeness, this intention behind all of nature that relies on subjective experience and consciousness, is quite different from the anthropomorphic images of God, religious doctrines that rely on law rather than nature's intention. For Dylan, the momentary place of God was in the falling. Now that he has learned how to fall, he has found the dance of fun and laughter. Since that day, he is fine and has never fallen since. For Dylan, the dance that incorporates both flying and falling is joy. For each of us, the problems that befall us are the gateway.

CHAPTER 5

One Plus One Plus One = One Dreaming "I"

In terms of time and dream research, Jung's theories have stood up, including, for example, the fact that all mammals dream, including infants, both in the womb and postnatally, and that the primary function of dreams is self-regulation and balance. Natural and compensatory, dreams are spontaneous, unadulterated symbols of the road to wholeness and transcendence. Jung devalued Freud's theory of dreams functioning to obfuscate and censor forbidden desire and emphasized instead the connection and synchronicity between inner and outer events.

Since Aristotle, philosophers have been interested in individuation. Jung, specifically, viewed this as a biological principle in all living organisms, his interpretation being that all living things are destined to become what they need to be, from the beginning. Thus, the big "I" becomes a creative act of Self-completion, an integration of the timeless Self with the time-bound personality of the contemporary man or woman. This occurs in a state of Self-mirroring and Self-witnessing. Jung further suggested that our difficulties come from losing contact with the age-old wisdom embedded within us.

Jung had his own concepts about gender differences: A believer in the alignment of opposites, he was clear about seeing sexual duality as parallel to the yin and yang in Taoist philosophy. Gender, he suggested, is the expression of the sex to which nature assigned us, established as early as eighteen months of age. Initially, it is the mother who is this carrier of the Self, for both boys and girls. For the girl, this presents no problem since she shares her gender consciousness with the equally shared identity with her mother; the boy, unlike the girl, has to make a transformation, based on his difference from the mother. Jung amplifies this theme by relating the girl/woman to Mother Earth, the creation of light out of darkness. Moving into mother-love, as distinct from father-love, he declares that mother-love is unconditional, it being sufficient for her that her child exists. Further, the Mother is an archetype found in Mother Nature, goddess of fertility, womb of life, and dispenser of nourishment. He states that girls tend to be more nurturant and affiliative than boys, seeking others and showing pleasure in doing so. Further, developing his principle of archetype, he created the theme of "animus" in women and "anima" in men, concluding that these internal contra-sexual opposites profoundly influence the relations of all men and women with one another, leading to "falling in love." He believed that the inferior feminine function in men is primarily feeling, symbolized by the female in men's dreams, and that the inferior masculine function in females is symbolized by masculine figures in their dreams. He found these symbols universal to all cultures. These figures indicate archetypal Self energies awaiting unfolding and conscious inclusion in the flow of life.

DREAMING FEMALE BIG "I"

Jodi, a forty-nine-year-old woman dreamt that she was swimming in the middle of the ocean. She saw a male swimmer that she associated with her husband. She was terrified to be in the ocean. Suddenly, she realized that she was all right by herself, that her swimming was natural and that she didn't need the man to save her. This was the first time Jodi felt this "all right" Big "I."

In the movie *The Swimming Pool*, Charlotte Rampling plays a woman whose esteem and strength are reliant on her male patriarchal publisher. Her writing style is also masculine, as if the man in her, and not she, is writing her detective novels. Often women dream that the man is driving their car. The Center shadow figure in the movie is the unexpected arrival of the daughter of her publisher. She is young, spontaneous, hungry, drunk, and full of life, sex, passion, and irresponsibility. Rampling's character is so bland, sober, and cold it hurts. In the movie, a young, renegade, irresponsible man is murdered. With the murder, the publisher's daughter also disappears. As the older woman integrates many of the younger woman's attributes and strengths, she begins to find herself and write from an earthy feeling and passion rather than intellect. That the events of the movie were the result of an active imagination rather than literal events becomes clear. Internally, Ms. Rampling drives her own car. Externally, she breaks away from her unhealthy reliance on her punitive and unrelated male publisher and becomes her own person, her own "I."

BREAKING THE SPELL—PERMISSION, REALIZATION

Cynthia was sixty when she dreamt the following: "I am lost. I want to get home. I approach a man who turns out to be a priest and ask him directions. He can't help. Still lost, I see another man, a well-dressed business man. I approach him and ask him if he can direct me home. He can't help either. Still lost, I approach a third man who looks like a professor. I ask him if he can direct me home. He can't. I realize that only I can find my way home."

This dream evokes the awakening of the "I" quest in the female. Native American women participated in quest rites of passage. Typically, the quest was undertaken alone and would occur in four stages. The task was to scale the mountain. Upon reaching the first stage of the journey, she would sacrifice all her material possessions. On the second stage, she would give up her friends and her community. On the third stage, she gave up her husband and her children. On the fourth stage, at the top of the mountain, it was just her and God. The fourth stage is an experience of totality, an incarnation of completeness. The experience of home, the essence of completeness within us.

Cynthia's reliance on the masculine other makes her lost. Her realization that "only I can find my way home" breaks the trance of her dependence. Caught in a spell of looking to a man for the answer, for his strength, for survival, for completeness, Cynthia remains secretly broken. Our most dangerous truth: that we are whole.

Those positive pseudo-clichés of our day—"total woman," "I see the divine in you," "you're perfect as you are"—that attest to our innate beauty and wholeness actually keep us from really taking the quest and making the necessary sacrifices to realize our completeness from within. Each sacrifice of an attachment is a form of death. Are we actually required to sacrifice everything to experience completeness? Are we responsible for experiencing our darkest fate? On an inner level, yes. On a ritual level, yes. On a feeling level, yes. With consciousness, we have the capacity to participate in every experience we need to grow, including dying. It's an inside job.

CYNTHIA'S "I" DREAM TEN YEARS LATER: RECONNECTING TO FEELING

"I am near a subway and meet a favorite aunt of mine and her daughter, my cousin (both deceased), and I'm thrilled to see them. We speak and reconnect. They are about to board a train, and they ask where I am going. I tell them that I will go with them since I so enjoy being with them once again. We board the train. After a short while, they get off to go home, and I get off with them but have to get to another train to get home. I do not know the trains nor do I have the proper change. A new system is in effect. I stop a young man and ask if he can change a bill for me. He gives me a bunch of change and won't take anything in exchange. He says 'keep it,' and I feel so pleased at how kind he is and accept. I board the first train that comes along but do not know if it is the right one. It is going someplace, and I am willing to go. On this train, I meet a young woman. She is very pretty, and we talk. She takes out a handful of chocolate-covered nuts and gives me some. I am again delighted with her kindness and the candies are delicious. I eat them. She gets off the train and I do too."

What does it mean to connect to the feminine? And, isn't a woman like Cynthia already there? Isn't what is considered feminine and what is deemed masculine a matter of culture, subjective opinion, and the prevailing wind of the day? By "feminine" we are not talking about the outer forms of behavior, beliefs, and cultural norms. We are referring to life force archetypal patterns, endowments, and functions that are universal in all cultures in both women and men. Internally and externally, we are energized by these forces as they are the nature of our nature. Archetypally, the feminine refers to our feeling function, our visceral experience and participation, our ability to receive, to be in the flow of our natural rhythm and nature, to reveal and express at the right time, love, nurture, and to be in the here and now. Metaphysically, "feminine" refers to our ability to be a vessel, to receive and mirror the light, for ourselves and for the world. Symbolized also by earth, the feminine refers to our capacity to hold a field where all worlds, all possibilities come together and revelation takes place.

The "masculine" refers primarily to our spirit, drive, thinking, and ordering function. Modern civilization has evolved around the masculine principle of thinking over feeling, order over spontaneity, detachment over passion, correctness over authenticity, passivity over conflict, extraversion over introversion, law over spirit, head over heart. Many symptoms, conflicts, and dramas of our day are driven by the disavowed natures in us that compel inclusion and refuse to be denied. Ten years prior, Cynthia broke the trance of her masculine reliance. What is masculine reliance? Externally, looking for the answer and completeness through a man; internally, relying on her rational thinking function only, rather than feeling, rhythm, and wisdom of the heart, body, and intuition. Now Cynthia's re-initiation to her feminine nature occurs.

MY HOME WITHIN: CYNTHIA'S
"I" REALIZATION OF INDEPENDENCE

"I realize I am in a neighborhood not far from my parents' home and reflect back that, in the old days, when my parents were alive, I could knock at any time. I also had my own key and could come in and stay. The house we had was big, roomy, and warm, but now they are gone, the house sold, and I can no longer go there. I'm all right anyway and say aloud that I will start to walk by myself and find a cab. I'm somewhat apprehensive since the neighborhood is very private and cabs not a usual thing. But I have enough money with me and begin the walk."

When Thomas Wolfe says "you can't go home again," he is referring literally to attempting to recreate our experience of "home." "Home" is an essence experience that is imprinted in every soul. We long for what is ours, and we get stuck in reenacting the outer forms, behaviors, people, and physical settings attached to the experience rather than the flow of its feeling and energy. Even if we have no physical history of having a home, we contain its imprint and desire. Some remain in life-long reaction to a nostalgic memory, never engaging in life, obsessed with retrieving what they lost, feeling cheated and envious of others who seem to have it. All essence experience comes from within and "home" is no different. Though repetitive reenactments take you to the precipice of the experience, the essence remains outside oneself, relent-lessly chased, compulsively driven, but ultimately lost.

The dream brings Cynthia back to the actual experience of home and the realization of the loss. Not the loss of "home" but the loss of at-tachment. "Home" she now experiences from within. Like the material attachments that were sacrificed during the Native American Quest, the physical forms, people, and images associated with "home" require sacrifice. The essence is "home," its feeling, energy, rhythm, con-stancy, and embodiment. Stuck in outer physical forms and memories, the essence "home" remains outside. Cynthia's Big "I" in the dream is experiencing that the flow of her Home essence is in her even though the physical forms and manifestations of the child home no longer ex-ist. "I'm all right." "I walk by myself." That Cynthia is energized by this "I" experience is indicated by the adequate money she has. She walks on her own individual power rather than using the collective vehicle, the cab. The energized, self-propelled walk reveals Cynthia's individuation, her "I" realization.

STUCK IN A ROLE

Phil is a forty-three-year-old professional actor who works hard on himself and his acting everyday. He dreams the following:

Part 1. "I'm paying off debts Carl has left behind. I don't mind. I'm pleased he left them organized and in such a way that made it clear what had to be done."

Part 2. "I'm going down a pretty suburban street. A good-looking, lanky black male starts to follow me. I think he will menace me. He seems to tackle me or trip me up and asks for my shoulder bag."

Phil says that he is the youngest brother of three and identifies him-self as the healer of the family. He's the one who sacrifices himself to keep things together. He's the only one who cares, the only one who sees what's going on. As long as he can remember, he has been rescuing his depressed mother and saving her from the evil, self-serving, unpredictable meanness of his father. Even today Phil feels responsible for making sure that his elderly mother is receiving the right treatment and that she is taken care of and not forsaken to die and be cheated by the father. Carl is the middle brother. Most of his life Carl withdrew and disappeared. The oldest brother, Andrew, who was actually physically and emotionally abused by the father, identified with his father, followed him in his profession, and became very aggressive. Recently, Carl, the middle brother, has become an invaluable ally and relieves Phil of many responsibilities and tasks that had been so consuming.

Internally, Carl is Phil's shadow. Externally he is his brother who withdrew and "took a powder." Phil's Carl image is a part of Phil that Phil does not identify as himself. Phil resents his brother's previous withdrawal and unavailability. Phil does not know this aspect in himself. The dream reveals a secret part of Phil that looks like Carl and that shows that something new is afoot. What is Carl's debt? And why does Phil not mind paying?

What is the dream trying to bring to light? In the first part of the dream, Carl's image is the Center of action. It has the most charge. After a lifetime of withdrawal, Carl now is the Center. Phil now associates Carl with actively helping. In describing Carl as a helper, Phil makes a small hand movement that emphasizes Carl's helpfulness. Encouraged to embody Carl's helpfulness, Phil first makes a facial gesture that fits Carl's attitude, then takes on Carl's helpfulness posture, then starts moving as Carl would move. Phil feels the energy immediately. "Carl nurtures." Carl's debt to Phil is the disavowed Carl-energy that this aspect of Phil keeps secret, that Phil does not identify within himself.

The difference in Phil between healing and nurturing is the difference between being stuck and enslaved in a role versus living his nurture essence. The nurturer in Phil is held in Carl's image. That is the Big "I" in this dream. Phil has been stuck in a role his whole life. He has literally martyred his life in this compulsive role. He never has a moment for himself. He is always in reaction to his unrelenting responsibility. He alone heals the others. But there is no one home (inside) for Phil. It is Phil's Big "I" that frees him, that gives him permission to have a "me," that supports him to be everything he can be. There is no conscious awareness in any role, just the drive to continue. It becomes the "devil you know," so familiar that it is scary to forsake even when you are called to live your true nature and desire. Roles are energized by archetypes and archetypal patterns within us. Roles organize around the shadow side of the archetype. The pure energy in Phil is Nurturing. That is his Big "I."

For Phil, the healer role was dreamt up, created by the field, atmosphere, and family he grew up in. He was compelled by vacuums (by what is not being expressed) and by the others who already occupied their roles and were able to express them more congruently than he could. Phil was unconsciously driven to express what was missing. Arriving as the Healer, he had no life of his own, no access to his own needs, his own real desire, his own destiny. If you look carefully, you might see the hidden essence of the Nurturer in Phil's healer role. But the Nurturer has an instinctual rhythm and song that is natural to Phil. The healer is a contrived, enslaving martyr adaptation with a secret envy that he can never be himself.

Phil's experience of himself as Nurturer breaks the spell of his embedded role and retrieves his nurturing essence in Carl's image. The dream brings together the two polarities of Carl's distancing and Phil's healer. Without breaking the spell and living through his Big "I" Nurture-essence, all Phil's relationships could revert around the familiar healer or its diametric polarity, the distancer. Now there is permission to live the archetypal essence that was hidden in shadow rather than be obligated, driven, and consumed by the role.

In the second part of Phil's dream, he feels menaced by a black male. "I'm going down a pretty suburban street. A good looking, lanky black male starts to follow me. I think he will menace me. He seems to tackle me or trip me up and asks for my shoulder bag."

Now the "lanky black male" takes Center. Phil's dark stranger is scary. Where is the ally in this stranger? The perceived enemy immediately initiates a clash by tackling or tripping Phil. One hint about the purpose of this enemy/ally: the shoulder bag in the dream refers to a burden, a personal cross to bear. When the "lanky black male" asks for the bag, we get a hint of an ally. But the dream leaves Phil under perceived attack. The wrestling or engagement with the "lanky black male" that already started in the dream can continue lucidly. The dream continues in the daytime. There is no diminution of the dream or of what is trying to occur.

Phil starts to move like the "lanky black male" in the dream and keeps it up; he starts with a menacing gesture and continues moving forward. In slowing down the movement, Phil feels its essence. He suddenly experiences something totally new, something his rational mind can't believe, so he stops. When he starts to move again the same way, it's confirmed. "It's easy." That is Phil's Big "I," Mr. Ease. That's what he called him. As a professional actor, Phil has trained in every technique imaginable. Desperate to find a technique that is close to his nature, he works hard with many teachers looking for the answer. Now he finds it in himself, held in the image of his "lanky black male," his ease, his rhythm.

In order to bring this down to earth, to live this in real life, there needs to be a pairing of both inspiration and implementation; otherwise, the Big "I" experience remains in potential, as a head trip or nostalgic memory. In order for a new reality to incarnate, it must be experienced in several facets or functions of our nature, in the parallel worlds within us. The different prayer modes reflect this: Some prayers are said individually, some together; some aloud, some silent; some in dialogue, some in song; some with eyes open, some with eyes closed; some with wine, bread, and food, some with movement. Actualization requires a totality of experience and the participation of all our worlds. Excluding one of our worlds is equivalent to disavowing a part of us or affronting a god. That was Pentheus's fate.

In ancient Greece, Pentheus was king of Thebes and grandson of Cadmus. As an enlightened powerful king, Pentheus worshiped only Apollo, who represented the rational, the sun, and the ability to wage and plan war and carve out control. When the time of year came to honor Dionysius (the God of spontaneity, wine, feeling, and ecstasy), Pentheus refused to participate in the rituals. The worshipers of Dionysius marching through the city, including Pentheus's sister and mother, were swept into a state of blind ecstasy that was part of the Dionysian ritual and they murdered Pentheus. In disavowing his feeling (feminine) and spontaneous nature, Pentheus was destroyed by the feminine (his mother and sister).

Apollo is the rational part of us; Dionysius, symbolizing feeling, passion, sensuality, and love, is disavowed by the order and structure of the rational. The murder of Pentheus, the rational, by the feminine of his family indicates the vengeance when one part of us is denied. The Big "I" includes both. The Big "I" needs participation and inclusion in all our worlds, in all our channels and functions, especially our inferior and neglected ones. What are the neglected functions of our era? Primarily feeling and relationship, our Big "I" essence experienced, revealed, and used for relationships. There is always an ordinary rational-mind boundary to being your Big "I," and always the certainty that the old established order will attack you from within for your being You. Especially at the boundary of using your Big "I" in relationship, in intimacy, and in the world.

Back to Mr. Ease. Phil starts to sing like Mr. Ease. He sings in his rhythm, natural, easy, free of technique. His lightness is contagious. Confident. Inviting. Awkward and shy, Phil now can use his ally "Mr. Ease" to engage, express himself, and guide him with others. That's why he's there, for Phil to be Phil.

JOHN'S DREAMING "I"

"I'm with my girlfriend at a club or restaurant. Mike, my friend, comes over and sits next to her. She responds to him immediately and they leave together."

John is twenty-nine, smart, introspective and passive. He is very polite and is constantly surprised and disturbed by assertive people. Mike has been a friend since high school and, says John, "he is like a magnet for all the girls." John is angry at Mike for his selfishness and instantly taking the center of attention in every social situation. John is awed by Mike's power and despises him for it. "Mike is evil."

Paralleling this situation, in the movie *Fight Club* there is a sequence of events where the same dynamic occurs. Ed Norton plays an overly civilized young man who takes no risks and endures a lot of abuse just to survive. Then the "evil" Brad Pitt enters his life. After his home is destroyed, Norton moves in with his new "friend" and a woman. Pitt and the woman connect instantly and go off for torrid sex together.

Norton, excluded, is left to himself. Eventually, Norton realizes that Pitt is really him and that he was the one actually having torrid sex with the female. As Norton becomes more conscious and integrates his evil Brad Pitt, his female partner transforms from a selfish hedonistic addict to a feeling and relating woman. They both grow. Norton becomes a whole person who is able to feel, respond, fight for himself and love. Excluded like Norton, John is about to realize that he's secretly Mike.

PERMISSION

John is very resistant to even imagining that any part of him is like Mike, but has no trouble making a gesture and movement that captures Mike's intrusiveness. The facial gesture is passive while the movement is fast and sneaky. John repeats these movements that simulated an actual experience where Mike grabbed a seat next to a woman that John was clearly headed for. At the point of speeding up like Mike, who had to get to the seat first, John experienced the energy in his body. "Its aggression." John leans forward when he says it. Encouraged to follow his forward direction, suddenly he says "go for it." Not a command, but a permission.

MEETING THE SHADOW AND ENGAGING TO GET ITS ENERGY

Now John senses his "go for it" energy. But he still feels excluded from its use. John's regular walking-around identity remains split from this essence. In his day-to-day-personality mode, John moves very fast. If we look at his movements, we see rushing. If we feel his movements, we sense fear. Over and over again, he rushes, as if he's running scared. How to integrate these two polarities, the "one-who-goes-for-it" essence and the "one-who-runs-scared" movement? That is the problem John must wrestle with. In the biblical story, Jonah is both the reluctant ally and the reluctant wrestler in us: As part of our highest nature, Jonah could be our greatest ally, but remaining stuck in his heavenly gaze, Jonah does not identify with us or feel our earthly sufferings. He does not identify with our mortal desires and fallibility. He runs from his earthly tasks and responsibility. This is represented by his sleeping in the heart of the vessel in the midst of a storm.

Why does John dream about Mike? Because like Jonah, John is reluctant to engage and wrestle. Mike is the part of John that "goes for it." John has disavowed a part of his essential nature that he needs to be whole and that is even now compelling expression. The dream image of "evil" Mike holds this disclaimed essence. The disturbing shadow figure takes the Center in John's dream and needs to be engaged to capture its hidden energy. That's where the action is, that's where the divine resides in the moment. Not in heaven, but in "evil" Mike. Only through participation and engagement with the Center does the hidden "I" essence experience of actually "going for it" become conscious, embodied, felt, and used in relationships. Stuck in Shadow, it would remain for others to act this out and for John to continue being victimized by his own hidden essence.

THE SUM OF "I"

Remember John, the twenty-nine-year-old man who experienced "Mr. Go For It?" He has had several Big "I" experiences since the first, each of which he has named: Mr. Go For It, Mr. Enthusiasm, Mr. Ahhh! John dreams: "I'm in a board room meeting. To my amazement, all those guys, Mr. Go For It, Mr. Enthusiasm, Mr. Ahhh!, and the others were all there. And they were cooperating with each other."

John has worked hard at using his revealed Big "I" essences in the world. He takes these experiences seriously and trusts them. John accumulates these Big "I" energies. There is a oneness in their diversity. They push his light beam forward until everything that John is becomes revealed, used, and embodied. Conjured up in the image of a board room meeting is an executive function of John's that brings these disparate capacities together, at least until he becomes his own double, his living energy, spirit-body, his fully incarnated Self, his embodied totality, side-by-side with his mortal self.

That is our direction. Do we actually achieve doubling? Every time we reexperience a Big "I" essence, bring it to consciousness, and use it in our world, we double. Self reveals. Our natural flow from source, Self, restores. We join our "I" individuation dream, our natural path consciously. Our real desire manifests. We live awareness and Self-reflection. We are not alone. That's what dreams bring. The possibility of participating in what's trying happen.

CHAPTER 6

Dancing with Shyness

At one critical point in his life, Jung underwent what he called his "creative illness." He associated this with experiences undergone by shamans, mystics, artists, writers, and philosophers. In treating one his patients, "Miss Miller," he detected a renunciation of the world, associated with an introversion and withdrawal of libido and interest in the outside world, followed by an acceptance of the world associated with an extraversion of libido, a more mature and participating adaptation to outer reality.

From this and the study of myth, philosophy, and religion, he concluded that two fundamental orientations exist: introverted and extraverted attitudes. Introversion is characterized by an inward movement of interest away from the outer world to the inner world of the subject; extraversion is characterized by an outward movement of interest away from the subject to the outer realm of objective reality. Jung believed himself to be an introvert, in opposition to Freud, from whom he had departed and whom he identified as an extravert. Due to this attention to his inner world, Jung retained a strong commitment to the life of the spirit along with his tendency to synchronize inner life with outer events and goals. Aware that every psychology has the character of a subjective confession, he recognized that, even when he was speaking or dealing with empirical, objective data, he was, in truth, speaking about himself.

Shyness is the shadow of our day. This is not a time of reluctance and hesitancy; instant participation is demanded. If you take a moment, you're dead. A sword of Damocles hangs in the air instigating instant response. Witness any board meeting, conflict forum, competition—the seemingly fittest are the loudest, fastest, most certain, and most extraverted. Overtly, the status quo drives everything. Where is there an honored place for imagination, creative experimentation, feeling insights, or deep truth? Where is the opportunity to have a dialogue and add different points of view? When the drama of competition is the end rather than the means, we are spellbound. Though socially acceptable in a layer of civility, we revert to a kill-or-be-killed, hunter/prey fixation. Identifying with the hunter rather than the prey is so enjoyable that we never find the secret of our wholeness that includes the prey.

HUNTER AND PREY

Prey is vilified. Worse, internally, it's relentlessly judged, criticized, and not accepted. In our culture, shyness is connected to being wounded, shutting down, going inside, being depressed. A suffering martyr? Or, a natural response against the stampede of certainty and immediacy? Pain brings a truth expressed by shyness that contradicts the tide of society's imperative for extraversion. But the shyness phenomenon also hides in plain sight, in counterphobic extraverted adaptations and expressions, in overt behaviors that are aggressive, confident, and manic.

When we are overdetermined in a response, as was Jasmine, "the fighter," what underlies that response is fear. For Jasmine, the fear was of being taken overtaken, demolished, trampled upon, made to disappear. All of this underlies the truth of her devastation—that she will no longer be, that she will cease to exist. To avoid this, Jasmine goes "overboard"—"I'll get you before you get me." But this in no way relieves her of the truth of her devastation. That young aspect of herself, stuck in early trauma, full of potential vitality and desire, is never accepted and lived.

Jasmine is the oldest of four sisters. She has been a fighter all her life. Overtly, she appears to be aggressive and confident and takes no bull. Exploration reveals a young, sensitive soul that is scared of being hit. She will always beat you to the punch. This is her counterphobic response to her devastation.

THE NEED FOR GROWN-UPS

Some counterphobic processes of our day can be seen in our children who suffer from Attention Deficit Hyperactivity Disorder (ADHD): aggression, competition, obesity, diabetes, autism, and early burn-out. Why? For one, we have a sibling society where parental roles remain in shadow. Father and mother grown-ups are a ghost in the background. As children, we expect our parents to be parents. Today's adults remain stuck in looking for the father, looking for the mother, who were supposed to be there. Or, they're renegades caught in eternal opposition to the parents. In either case, there's nobody home but children pretending to be grown-ups. With no sense of home and pretense of adulthood, fear rules.

There was a time when our parents were "Oedipal-worthy;" that is they carried the image of the adequate mother/father. When we as children lost to these images, losing to their adequacy and strength, we simultaneously internalized them. It was our necessary loss, to them that returned us to the flow of our childhood essence and added the protection and acceptance of internalized adults in our backgrounds. These adults were not perfect, but, still, they were adequate adults.

With Freud, the Oedipus complex became a major theme in psychology/psychotherapy—"work it through" and your analysis is complete. What is the Oedipus complex? For Freud, in a nutshell, it was boys being in love with their mothers and jealous of their fathers. In his view, the boy child is interested in the mother and also wants to take possession of her, and he is thus hostile to his father and assumes the father will retaliate, a form of castration. Through the process of the Oedipal complex, the boy finally gives up all hope of sexual union with his mother, identifies himself with his potentially aggressive father, and finally turns his attention toward getting sexual satisfaction from other sources. Freud believed that because girls are without a penis, they must have already suffered castration. He believed that the girl child, finding she lacks a penis and that she is therefore inferior, blames the mother, moves toward her father as love object, and imagines he will make her pregnant, which is compensation for not having a penis. What then? She seeks other men who will impregnate her, she will have a baby, and, thereby, she overcomes her sense of being an inferior kind of human being.

Jung's interpretation was very different from that proposed by Freud. In his view, a child attaches to his mother not because she is the object of incestuous passion but because she is the provider of love and care. Jung stated that the Oedipus complex was not the universal phenomenon that Freud declared it to be. The myth reflects the modern civilized dilemma of science and rational thinking at the expense of inner experience. The myth ends with Oedipus at peace with his state of blindness, reflecting introversion, the counterbalancing attitude that makes him whole.

At forty-seven, Greg dreamt that he was asleep in the bedroom where he slept when he was fourteen. Suddenly, he heard a great crash. Jumping out of bed, he ran to his parents' bedroom to see if they were okay. He was astonished to find his parents' beds pulled together and to see them lying naked, glistening from sex freshly consummated. That was his dream. To Greg, the idea of his father's potency and sexuality was foreign to him. He had never lost to an adequate father. We are programmed to lose. Without loss, there is no father and the child rules. Sometimes he/she becomes a Giant. But the calmness and adequacy of the father and the love of the mother is never internalized. Greg experienced the adequacy of his father at age forty-seven, at which time his own children were already grown. Greg represents a biological adult in our society whose internal experience was like that of an orphan, the sense of being alone, having nobody home, and being overwhelmed.

The necessary loss gets postponed, past childhood, past adolescence, past adulthood, into the second half of life. We inherit a kingdom that requires no struggle and no losses. We remain in the entitlement of that kingdom without struggle. Avoiding fate, we obtain a relinquished kingdom of our making. We occupy a house that we haven't earned or bought, with no grownups.

Lightning strikes. Vacuums are filled. The disavowed essence energies, unmirrored, fragment into their opposite components, wide extremes of attributes, beliefs, behaviors and problems diametrically opposed to the sanctity and safety of the established order. Secret, dangerous, devastating, powerful, and ghostly, they are both threatening and mystifying. An unrestricted, extreme, polar opposite version of our sense of control. These, the unexpressed sides of this kingdom without struggle, pain, or loss, are compelled to be expressed, with a vengeance.

Cheating fate, evading loss, avoiding struggle, depth, and contradiction, we have evolved into a nation of bourgeois smart-asses: fat, lazy, pseudo-hunter predators, not ready for our inevitable turn as prey. Our vital instincts are subdued in the service of cultural ideals of no struggle, no war, and rational brilliance. After all, to date, we've never risked or lost anything. Our expansive instinct for love, inclusion, awareness, consciousness of others, and responsibility still lands at adolescence but remains in the background, a perpetual contradiction to the culture of certainty. We know something is wrong, we sense it all around, but we're too busy surviving. Even in the midst of prosperity and privilege, there is little but survival. People identify with those above them, with little love or empathy for those below.

Take a three-day conference on discrimination: On the first day, it's the women's turn. They express outrage against two thousand years of suppression and victimization. Day two focuses on gay people. The women hardly show up. You might think that they naturally empathize with homosexuals. Absolutely not. The third day it's the African Americans' turn. Do you think the gays think about the African Americans? Or do the women? Of the many reasons why the Soviet Union and communism collapsed, the idea that a proletariat exists as adversaries to the owners of the means of production was the greatest delusion; instead, people measured themselves by the owners and their rewards and wanted to be them.

Without integrating a natural archetypal order starting with parents, we remain stuck in predatory competition as either hunter or prey. No love, no higher purpose drives us, just hunting, taking, and self-feeding without any of the spiritual awareness, purposefulness, sacrifice, or restriction of the hunting traditions of our ancestors. Who would have imagined that railing about our entitlement, our democratic rights, and our victimization would become such a self-feeding frenzy? Democracy's own tyranny that imitates struggle. Like Pentheus, who by worshiping only Apollo and refusing Dionysius brings about his own destruction, whatever god we deny, whatever process we avoid, whatever aspect of ourselves we disown, comes back with a vengeance.

Abraham is known for arguing with God about the fate of Sodom and Gomorrah. A hidden truth about Sodom and Gomorrah is that Abraham was responsible for its destruction. How? Abraham split from his brother Lot after a disagreement. Lot went to settle in Sodom. Abraham knew that his decision to part resulted in the destruction of Sodom and Gomorrah. When we disavow an aspect of ourselves, there is always a destruction. We have a heavenly level in us to experience death, loss, and destruction, through which we can learn and grow. When this process does not occur, the experience occurs in the here-and-now on earth—physical death. We have no current communal rituals or rites of passage that access these experiences that bring us to our fate.

SHYNESS ERUPTS

The world's first shy person? Jung cites a writing dated approximately 2600 BCE in Egypt, called "A World Weary Man in Search of His Ba" (*ba* means soul). In it, a man recorded a spontaneous eruption of conscience and contradiction. Overwhelmed by the meaninglessness of life, the selfishness, banality, avarice, superficiality, absence of love, materialism, and his alienation, he intended to follow hordes of others of his time and commit suicide. This was the prevailing behavior of the time, the only known reality. Suddenly, he heard a voice embracing the value of his life.

This was unheard of in the ancient world: a second voice, a contradiction, questioning the established order, accessing a level beyond the known. These did not exist. The ancient world knew fear but not shyness. Shyness denotes a reluctance, being caught between two contradictory oppositional forces, "yes" and "no." Overtly, shyness looks like giving up and being overwhelmed. Afflicted by shame, wounded, our culture pays homage to free choice and self-determination but actually abhors free will. The culture demands its rules and certainties be followed. "No" is not acceptable unless it is culturally prescribed. So, we fall into lockstep with the collective, participate and function in it, bask in its applause and glory and all seems okay.

Frances, a thirty-two-year-old single professional joins a group of fellow young professional adults. Two years later, she complains that all the others in the group seem to be getting better except her. "They came in confused, troubled, and lost. Now, everything for them is getting better." What was the magical cure? They became their parents. What was the key to their transformation? They gave up their own track, their own dance that was alive and well in their problems, disturbances, and malfunctions.

Overtly, they fit in. Secretly, they gave up. As an outsider who remained oppositional and defiant, it was automatic for Frances to envy the ease with which everything became OK for her peers. This is the collective Band-Aid of modern life: fit in, play by the rules, ignore your subjective experience. Struggle is not required. Be smart. The rules have remained the same since Job's comforters told him to ignore his truth. Repent. Follow your truth and you will die. Your safety lies in the certainty of the established order, not your truth, not your experience, not your real desire. Your life and your strength is in society's dictates.

So what do we do when our personal truth contradicts the collective tide? How do we shut down or bring choice to the riptide of extraversion, "shoulds," and "supposed tos"? Shyness expresses our second reality, our reluctance, our shame, our contradiction. Big secret: Shyness contains our big "no," our free choice stuck in a spell of shyness. One would never know that, unfolded, shyness holds our real power. That first unearned victory is secretly traumatic; the natural order is to lose to the grown-ups. When the grown-ups are defeated, we're defeated. Because we're also the grown-ups. We spend a lifetime looking for the grown-ups or mesmerized by the power in the repetition of defeating them or in the orphaned spell of defeat. The grown-ups remain in shadow until the second half of life when our problems and symptoms can no longer be denied. Unfolded, these processes yield big essence allies that are our adults.

Peter, thirty-three, manages his family business. He complains of chronic trouble managing his workers. He says that every time he tells someone what to do, they hate him. If he acts strong or speaks his mind to a worker, to a friend, to a family member, or to anybody for that matter, he is hated. He believes that just by approaching somebody he initiates hate. Even though he feels it's no use, Peter experiments with all kinds of engagement strategies, but then gives up at the first perceived rejection.

Peter faces an atmosphere of hatred every time he walks into a social encounter. This is his repetitive reality with another: hatred waiting for a place to happen. Shy, awkward, and judgmental about his own perception, Peter says, "I'm contaminated." Taking his reality seriously, Peter expresses the hatred and disdain that is coming at him. What is going on inside Peter at that moment? Peter speaks about anger and frustration and demonstrates these feelings by holding his body tight, clenching his fists and bringing them to shoulder level. At that point, he gives up by slackening his posture completely. When asked whether he gave up, he says without flinching, "Yes. It's no use, you see." Encouraged to really give up, he says, "I don't want to." On his own, Peter returns to the posture with his fists clenched directly above his shoulders. Encouraged to follow the movement and bring his arms and fists back to where they want to go, he does so and smiles. "I can say anything to anybody in this position. I can be direct." Peter's truth, permission, and choice are embodied in this figure, his first authentic "yes" or "no," his real ally and protector, the conscious, awakened parent we all need. The problem of shyness holds Peter's essence, his largest nature which is, in actuality, directness.

Peter could spend an eternity seeking the answer to "why," never integrating the archetypal essence behind this image of hatred. Peter's daily nightmare of being hated holds the energy of his "directness," his secret relationship-maker. Fragmented and distorted in the image of hatred, Peter would inevitably be drawn by compulsion to reenact this drama to make him whole. In directness Peter expresses what he feels. By saying his truth in the moment, he takes his power. He then has permission to receive, to participate in life, to enjoy others, to say "yes" and "no," to have a "me."

Rita, a well-established mental health professional, has spent twenty-five years working on herself along with her clients. Very together, articulate, and sophisticated, she has achieved a substantial following. Rita is known for never being at a loss for words. But suddenly her world changed. Realizing she has been living a lie, that the face she showed the world was not her own, she feels devastated, naked, and shy. Rita was faced with the loss of her best friend, who threatened to leave her if she continued a relationship with a man whom the friend knew was only about money, and this broke the spell of Rita's façade.

Now defenseless and exposed, Rita has become shy in public. Where before she had no hesitancy to express herself, now she can barely get a word out. "I feel judged. I know it's my mother, criticizing. I'm scared to talk." Asked to show a gesture of the judge's attitude, she says, "That's easy to do," and makes a discarding motion with her hand, like someone dismissing another. She then pauses and says, "Wait. This is better," and makes a strong kicking "get-away-from-me" movement with her leg. Asked to repeat the kicking gesture, but more slowly, she stops after the third repetition and says, "I think I've given up." But as she's saying this, her head is going back and forth in a constant "no" motion. Asked whether she's aware of what she's doing, she says, "No. I'm not aware that I am doing it." Encouraged to exaggerate the head motion, she does, and then she looks up in realization and says, "I can say, 'No.'"

The shadow figure of the mother criticizing, the energy of the judge in it initially looks horrible to Rita. She doesn't know or see these negative attributes in herself. Now, at her door, they cause her pain, not realizing these are her own energies at work. By kinesthetically joining these energies, she experiences their intent, which is nothing short of breaking the trance of her robotic existence, a new consciousness, where choice exists and where desire and heart are accepted.

THE POWER OF SHYNESS

Shyness holds the antidote to being devoured by the mother, the father, the culture, the tribe. Gravity is such a natural force that we hardly notice its presence; its pull is constant. Like gravity, misery, self-pity, and pity of others operate on us from behind, a secret death agenda camouflaged in social rules, nonconflict, and correctness. No risk, no heroism, no real desire is allowed; shyness holds our fire, our reluctance "to go gentle into the good night."

Shyness has become pathologized. Pills for shyness proliferate. Diagnoses of social anxiety justify medication; in some public schools, up to 80 percent of the children are diagnosed with Attention Deficit Hyperactivity Disorder (ADHD) and are under medication; one out of 156 children show autism; childhood obesity is epidemic; a generation of lost boys and girls, introverted and feeling rather than thinking and extraverted, fall way behind in reading and math. From a shyness point of view, this makes sense. As parents forsake their roles, there is no protection against the frenetic pace of life, the unabated stimulation, the absence of boundaries between grown-ups and children, and the manic-driven, extraverted, no-shame behaviors.

Children pick up and automatically mimic the charged, disturbing, incongruent, and incomplete expressions of their parents. No shame. No mercy. No protection. Pure judgment. Without awareness, we martyr ourselves. We try to fix first our parents then the world by expressing what is disavowed, forbidden, or incongruent in the other. Unintentionally, we voluntarily embody what is in shadow, what is missing, what is secret or not fully expressed, what is one-sided, what is charged, and what is disturbing, both good and bad. We are pushed to complete the partial expression, to express the disturbing nature more fully, more directly, and more congruently. That's how our children take over and hold our most disturbing facets. That's how consciousness is held, how revelation awaits.

Meredith, forty-one, is married to George, forty-five, and they have two children, Mark, seven, and Stacy, five. Both parents are very extra-verted; both work. Their life races from one frenetic activity to another. The children have no free time; every moment is scheduled. From the beginning, the children, both adopted, are the constant center of atten-tion. Dreams, hopes, gifts, activities, conversations, nonstop presents, indulgences. The parents seem to live vicariously through the children to a degree not seen in generations before. There are few boundaries between parents and children. Every night the parents share their bed with their children. Bedtimes don't really exist. The atmosphere is one of nonstop involvement, with no quiet time, no parallel play. The children are demanding, and somehow the parents seem to like it that way. When the mother describes the children's demanding nature, she smirks a secret smile of approval. Parental involvement is nonstop. Both children can't focus, both are hyperactive. Both act out within a moment of noninvolvement. Both can't stop. They are diagnosed with ADHD.

Jung said that children are compelled to live the unlived life of their parents. Living out their parents' shadow, the unlived life of parents today that is being expressed is adulthood. Rejecting adulthood, parents today identify with their children and live vicariously through them. Admiration (rather than acceptance) and competition, envy, and annihilation (rather than authority and responsibility) rule. How did this come about? The baby-boomer generation (born 1946–1965) were products of parents galvanized by the Great Depression and World War II. Their parents' lives were marked by participation in cataclysmic history and personal sacrifice. They grew up fast, entering an age of responsibility and grown-up behaviors. What they left behind—their childhood—their children of the late 1940s, 1950s, and 1960s, lived out.

Stuck in the inalienable right and dream of childhood, privileged Peter Pans, spiritually awakened in the 1960s, only to retreat to the materialism of their parents tenfold, yet still fixed in childhood, they are the parents of today. What is their shadow? What is unlived? Do the aggressive, hyperactive, entitled, tyrannical, enraged, and terrorizing behaviors we are now witnessing reveal a missing essence? For one, it's the strength and the role of the grown-up. We know this by observation of families who have children with problems. When parents resume their adult roles, when competition and conflict between the parents is amplified and openly expressed, children resume their individual nature and roles as children. Symptoms are reduced and natural order is restored. It takes a grown-up to penetrate this enmeshment. With adults in the closet, the world is unsafe. There are no restrictions or boundaries: some children plunge into acting-out, others to acting-in. One child responds with aggression and hyperactivity, another withdraws.

A civilization, family, or environment in act-out mode is devastatingly intrusive. Some join the mob. Shyness is our instinctual reluctance to join the stampede. Yet, shyness is not the antidote to an extraverted false self. We can also make a god out of shyness itself. In truth, we can make an addiction out of anything, And we do. Shyness itself is so powerful that it becomes the great determiner of modern civilization. That's what addictions are for.

Take John: Now forty-one, he repetitively makes eye contact with young men while traveling the subways. Instantly, he knows and motions to the other. They get off the train together, go to John's apartment, and have quick sex. They never see each other again. John seems like a typical shy, sensitive male, and you would never suspect his predatory, aggressive, and often ruthless nature. John takes the lead. When his look is mirrored, he's home. Confidence reigns. He feels permission to take, without restriction, guilt, or ambivalence. This is quite a contradiction to the shy, delicate, caretaking persona he presents. John carries out this dangerous agenda once a week. He's scheduled. When John's friend says, "There's no intimacy in this," John responds, "That's the idea."

John seduced his first Adonis at seventeen. From that moment on, he felt okay. All his self-consciousness disappeared. He now felt worthy, beautiful, sure, and potent. Cured. That overwhelmed boy who worshipped his mother and repeatedly saved her from her depression and her abusive husband, a never-ending task requiring his total hypervigilance and sacrifice, stopped. Finally, he could take something for himself and not apologize. Except that this experience was caught in the image of John's behavior and act-out. It's as if it happens outside of John, stolen rather than earned. The baseline is still shame. But who cares, when instant wholeness is one action away, the answer to life? That is the secret behind every addiction. It's not you. It's "it." The high dream behind the addiction, the experience of wholeness, the missing attribute, remains outside. What is the high dream? When John is on the hunt, his eyes open, body lengthens, jaw squares, and alertness springs. Totally focused and serious, John's determination is contagious.

Holding the position of hunter-predator, John says, "I feel like Donald Trump." What is John's biggest problem? "My shyness. Being taken seriously." Imagine having a Trump-like essence! John, making a Trump-like gesture, stands tall, regal, confident, and totally at ease. Now, as shyness takes a turn, John hides his face. With Trump and shyness, we could not get two more separate worlds. Yet, these two worlds make one totality. Our delusion is in keeping them separate. Experimenting with each gesture to find the movement, dance, or image that is true to both worlds, John alternates between regality and hiding. He moves around, going from one gesture to the other, until he finds a dance. A dance of carefulness, awareness, and concern for others. John then demonstrates his daily personality: shy, scared, tentative, desperate to say the right thing, hiding a constant rage and frustration. Hyper-vigilant, John walks. You can feel his aloneness.

Than he switches. Now he embodies his careful, caring essence, and the therapist starts to walk around as John's everyday shy aloneness. Will these worlds ever come together? Remaining alone for a seeming eternity, the therapist wonders whether a caring John will ever notice. John is at the therapist's back. His therapist expects nothing. Shy John is used to being alone. Suddenly, Caring John approaches, embraces and supports the therapist's back, encouraging the acceptance of his guidance and saying that he is there for the therapist. Feeling this to be right, the fear, the aloneness, gone. We switch. John now beginning to walk in his shy aloneness, the therapist holding Careful-Caring John. Supporting and guiding John, embodying his caring essence, John now feels joy and wants to explore. We experiment approaching people and interacting with them, Little John's curiosity with Big Careful John as guide. What a difference an essence makes! The dream behind John's addiction is nothing less than his High Self ally and guide, the missing Real Parent in our world.

It's the combination of Predatory John with Shy John that reveals Caring John. Brought together, they create a wholeness, a restoration of natural order that breaks the trance of inadequate alones. By including the seeming separate energies inside ourselves, we become who we really are and what we have always been.

CHAPTER 7

Shadow in Relationships

Carl Jung said, "Everything that irritates us about others can lead to a better understanding of ourselves." During Jung's lifetime, university psychology departments were dominated by behaviorism, stressing behavioral techniques and banning the unconscious psyche and introspective techniques. By contrast, Jung stressed inner events, insisting that the psyche and its study through introspection and personal experience took precedence above all else. Jung claimed that it was our innate propensities that provide the basis for all psychological knowledge and experience. For him, Western society, detached from its Judeo-Christian roots, was materialistic, spiritually impoverished, and technologically obsessed. This leads us to treat each other as economic commodities, exploiting the physical resources of the planet while neglecting the spiritual resources of the Self. The remedy for this loss of soul was nothing less than a reinvestment in the inner life of the individual, so as to reestablish a personal connection with the mythic world where we are at home, by right of birth, and without which we are cut off from vitality, meaning connection. Jung deeply felt that the quest for the cosmic connection, the experience for the Holy and the Sacred, was the fundamental parallel to the Self. To deny it brings spiritual decay; to embrace it illuminates the soul with meaning.

Stuck in the romantic millennium, we expect everything from parents, friends, partners, and lovers. Seeing God in the other has become our national pastime. Secret emptiness charged by the image of others, it provides pseudo-love, acceptance, understanding, mirroring, and wholeness outside one's self. To be impacted by its delusion and loss impels the search for the Self. Replacing the narrow view of the collective that sees our task as security, certainty, and the cessation of conflict, in the search for Self we discover that the true purpose of life is to serve our mystery through living our own unique pattern, imprinted at birth.

WE ARE ALL BORN TWINS

Remember Esau? The first-born of the twins in us? We are all born twins. Like Esau, the first-born is a "hunter." The processes of our early life—attachment, survival, adaptation to our environment—require a hunter. Remember Lucy and her glorious story nature? Her teacher rejected this part of herself, so for that world, she became what was expected of her. A "face," a persona that was accepted. Her authentic story nature was disavowed in the service of fitting in and being applauded.

She became a hunter, a civilized predator of fitting in and getting accolades. As hunter, the distinction between hunter and hunted prey blurs. To kill or be killed is ever-present. What looks like love is instinctual attachment and vulnerability. Socialization hunts you down: secretly, we hunt back. When we are mirrored, accepted, and loved, we respond well. Our hunter instinct finds what it needs in our self and in others.

The Kabbalists see life as a battle within us, our own civil war between our first-born hunter and the subsequent aspect of love, relatedness, and responsibility that incarnates around age thirteen. The hunter connects to the desire to receive for the self alone. With the expansion of consciousness that occurs in adolescence comes the desire to receive for the sake of sharing. Traditionally, the biological emergence of sexual maturity in both men and women indicated their readiness for mature responsibility and taking an appropriate role in the community. But there was always immersion in rite-of-passage rituals that enabled the new reality to become home. Emerging from these rites you were no longer your mother's beautiful golden boy or girl. In these rituals, you participated in your own death. What died was the immature part of you, the self-absorbed, self-centered part; now this center of the universe sense goes into the background, taking second place to the new reality: love, relatedness, awareness, responsibility, community, and the path of the heart.

Archetypal Self images such as Queen, King, Mother, Father, and Warrior refer to this nature: Buddha consciousness, Christ consciousness, Higher Self, personify this reality. What does this higher nature hold that our hunter is devoid of? The path of the heart. Love. Acceptance. Permission. Detachment. Choice. What does this have to do with relationships? Our Highest Self is the shadow of every relationship, our biggest "I." Popular culture has embraced the idea of the inner child. The problem isn't the child, it's spitting out an adult. Our Big "I," in all its aspects, is our adult. Unlike our predecessors, we are not prepared by contemporary celebrations, confirmations, or communions of the day for our new reality.

We have no container for our first experience of real love, that initial spontaneous archetypal energy and experience that includes all of life, that wonderful instant of whole-making, life-changing experience that makes everything right. Without the merciful rite of dying-into-life experience, our embedded hunter/prey/survival reality comes back with a vengeance. Then the essence experience, love, becomes secretly stored in a complex of behaviors, images, rules, roles, addictions, and unconscious bonding patterns. Yet, the image of the other, no matter how far the relationship has distanced from love, still holds our essence, our biggest "I." Accept that many of the images and repetitive behaviors associated with love are culturally acceptable. Where has love gone? It hides in plain sight, in culturally permissible relationship behaviors, entitlements, expectations, verbalizations, relationship rules, and demonstrations of love.

DEALING WITH OUR DISAVOWED ESSENCE

How do we master the pain and loss of our disavowed essence? A week before her wedding Sophia dreamt that "I entered a Cathedral Church to attend a wedding. The reception was located near the entrance. I went inside and noticed a hidden entrance leading to a secret passage, which I followed. The secret passage took me to the inner sanctum of the church. I entered a great hall where a magnificent wedding was taking place. I realized that this was the real wedding."

The dream makes the distinction between the superficial—pretend—wedding near the entrance and the real essence marriage hidden within. The dreamer realized the implication of the dream, that she was going to participate in a surface wedding, but she went through with her actual wedding anyway. One year later, the marriage was annulled. The real wedding came later. The essence experience, the "real marriage," must come from within, must be known from within, and not just an outer form, an "as if" ceremony.

We act "as if" we come from love and from our higher consciousness and intent. We talk homage to love. That way the Big "I" of love continues to hide in plain sight, politically correct and outside ourselves. While we talk of love, we remain hunters. We become prey. Without our Big "I" essence we revert to a sibling society of hunter and hunted. No adults. No one watching the store. Only hunters playing at adulthood and adult games with no love, consciousness, relatedness, natural order, or courage. No eldership. No accumulation of experience. Just consumption. It is our Big "I" that is our adult, our mirror, and our ally.

Put two Big "I's" together and a "We" is possible. Anything is possible. Intimacy is possible. Love is possible. New is possible. Put two hunters together. Only prey and ashes are possible until the wound is felt, experienced, and made meaningful, rather than reenacted. Then and only then does the Big "I" emerge. All routes lead to the Self—even the destructive ones. The Big "I" behind the Noncouple Couple.

Paula dreamt:

I'm away from home with my husband. The surroundings are beautiful. Mountains, sunlight. Just lovely! Max, my husband, and I are in bed together. We have been married for a few years, a so-so marriage, like lukewarm milk. Nothing to get excited about. We held off having kids. In bed that night as with many others, nothing was happening. On the bed near us, I could see a couple rolling around, she large and blonde, he unseen. They were laughing a lot and were having a great time. Max left. I felt alone. Suddenly, someone was in bed with me. A man. I didn't know where he came from. It seemed almost like he had always been there, just not noticed. He turned to me with interest. He moved toward me and then cupped my breast in his hand, which, though surprised, I allowed. I wondered if he would think me beautiful. I was not large like the blonde near me but rather small, slim, and dainty. He caressed my breast. I held my breath waiting for his response. "You are so very lovely. Your breast is small, firm, and uplifted like a young girl." His hand went to my vagina, and he spoke softly. "You are ready for me." Flooded with pleasure but staying in the moment, I realized I had not told him I was married. I decided not to. He was a large, solid man. He then said, "We can go off on a trip together and since they have seminars for all of us, I wonder if you are in some of mine? Are you interested? I hope we can be in some classes together." I stayed quiet and wondered if it was time to leave my marriage. Perhaps the time was now. With him. A new calm and joy settled on me.

Isn't it amazing that people are still pairing off? Expectations of beauty, joy, fun, togetherness, and desire for relationship persist. Is pairing driven by an ever-present stigma of failure and incompleteness, of not being in a beloved relationship? Both myth and literature indicate that love is tragic. Jack Benny said, "You should always marry an ugly woman because a pretty woman can leave you. Well, an ugly woman can leave you, too, but who cares?"

Remember the *Narnia Chronicles,* where the established order is ruled by the tyrannical Ice Queen, and the new kingdom of love, joy, and heart is set off somewhere on the periphery? That's where Paula and Max live, in the tyranny of the Ice Queen, settling for the crumbs of their lukewarm existence. They see the purgatory of their blandness in each other's eyes. On the bed next to theirs lies the answer to life, seemingly. The large, blonde, full-of-life woman and her fun-loving male partner are quite the fiery contradiction to Paula and Max. Does every bland couple have a fiery couple in the closet? And is the fiery couple the goal? What does the revelation of this second couple foretell? That a third reality lurks. What happens when we identify as one of the first two couples? We relapse into chronic repetition of being stuck in their polarity. We revert to being lukewarm milk and seeing this in the other. Or we find a boyfriend/girlfriend that fits the fire and disavows our own lukewarm nature or puts it on the other. Poor Max, he loses either way. Or the couple reverts completely to fire and the spell of desire. Living as one pole or the other never accesses the dance between the two poles or the lurking third big-reality myth underneath. Can Paula and Max integrate this fiery couple? Is this going on just inside Paula or in both Paula and Max?

From Paula's perspective, she is stuck with Max. When Paula is with Max she is lukewarm. This has become her reality, the devil she knows. Paula and Max must separate, leave to make room for the other. Internally, Paula's inner masculine fixates on Max's image. Now that he leaves and she enters the unknown of her loneliness, her inner masculine can resume his flow of life, no longer stuck as Max. Paula has made room for a new inner other. Like Paula, who entered an abyss of aloneness in the absence of Max, we in our lives can rejoin the flow of our nature by detaching from the set image of the other, through the "I" of being alone, through surviving by ourselves. That is the sacrifice: the loss of the small "we," the "we" without an "I," the "we" of eternal loneliness, eternal drudgery, the "we" without an adult, love, awareness, completeness. No love. No awareness. No completeness. Two children/hunters remain in a hedonistic fantasy of raw survival driven by secret envy of their own hidden shadow, the small "we" of our enslavement, blame, and seeing your inadequacy in the other.

The cure for the "we" of eternal loneliness always remains on the horizon, stuck in the "we" of being less than whole. Who tells us we are anything less than beautiful? Cheryl, a thirty-eight-year-old, middle-class, married, African American woman provided a glimpse into this spell. A fire-cracker, engaging personality, Cheryl lit up any doorway she entered. By day, she acted as a conventional suburban homemaker. By night, she was a shrewd, tough-as-nails crack addict who supported her addiction by operating a seemingly legitimate nonprofit charity of which she was, of course, the only beneficiary. During her addiction treatment, one of Cheryl's male peers told her, "All you really need is to be with a man like me." Without blinking, Cheryl said, "Robert, you wouldn't last three minutes." What is Cheryl saying? "You have no power. You're nothing. I'm impervious to your impact and proud of it. Nothing and no one will affect me. I'm invulnerable." What was the shadow hidden behind Cheryl's impervious declaration? "God forbid you should ever be impacted or penetrated by anyone." Those were the words spoken to Cheryl that joined the denied and unspoken desire. They affect her to this day.

Ancient teachings refer to an invisible shield around the heart. The second half of life is set up to break this force-field. The heart needs to be pierced so that its energy and real desire can flow free, so that we can feel, love, and be penetrated. We need to experience the newness and awesomeness of life, and of each other. Nature's paradoxical gift is that when we are impacted we have impact. Upon impact, the dance of life and caring resumes. Are you strong enough to be vulnerable, to be mortal, and to know the impact you have? Are you available to be felt and affected by the other?

Paula senses the presence of the new man who has always been there. This masculine other relates and responds. He is touched by Paula. Paula is not used to being felt, to having an impact. Like Cheryl, she is used to the numbness of having no impact, of not being affected by or affecting the other. Self-conscious and self-critical, at the edge of the new experience, lie the collective imperatives, the rules of the established order. "Confess the marriage. How dare you?"

Despite this, Paula consciously decides to proceed with the experience. Penetration occurs. A "We" is born. What makes this "We" different from the old "we?" When the stranger from the other bed tells Paula that he hopes they can be in some classes together, that indicates that the one-or-the-other diametric polarity between the small "we" of indifference and the unconscious "we" of pure fire no longer rules. There is a We and a Not-We. Two individuals, two Mortals on earth, touched by each other, accepting of each other, sharing a relationship, sharing love. "Calm and joy." Paula's Big "I." A We of two "I's." And what about Cheryl?

Several years later, Cheryl, appeared on a nationally syndicated TV show telling her story. Afterward she said that she had returned to her husband, who previously had a distinct similarity to Paula's "lukewarm Max." Softly Cheryl continued, "Now I'm a bride for the first time." The core We is two Big "I's," not an enmeshment, but an addition. The idea of a We made of two or more Big "I's" is a Big "WE."

The unconscious compensatory bonding patterns we are used to, the secret deals, are compelled to disappoint and wither. Behind attributing completeness to, in, or with the other, lurks a Big "I." Our Individuation is a sum game and adding the relationship big "I" is our program. The pierced heart foretells the inner marriage. It is then that the inner

marriage becomes actualized in a Big WE, not before. Society ritualized this inner marriage through conventional, formal marriage cer-
monies. Today the outer form, conventional marriage, is far removed
from its original spirit and truth. We presume that this special We is in
everybody and readily available. By the wedding date an assumption
prevails that this Big WE exists, that the inner wedding has already occurred. This is a dangerous projection in an age of act-out and minimal
restriction where projecting this Big "I" onto the other is loaded with
disappointment and possible disaster.

THE HIGH DREAM BEHIND ROMANCE

➤ "Religion is for people who don't want to go to hell. Spirituality is for
people who've been there." Go to any twelve-step program and you are
likely to hear this spoken. It implies that until you have been impacted
by life, by addiction, by fate, by love, by suffering, you have no ap-
preciation of your mortal soul. You remain stuck in a kind of rational
hubris that uses words, laws, opinions, and dramas to nullify and avoid
experience. Like Sophia in her dream about the real inner wedding, we
participate in a lot of surface weddings and relationship interactions
that imitate but don't access the essence experience and the path of the
heart.

Are we rehearsing to enter a dream-gate of real experience or ce-
menting the established order? What happens when you fall in love or
actualize a dream with a real-life counterpart, when you experience a
state of "we" that feels perfect with a human being, a drug, an activity,
a fantasy? All these participate in High Dream spontaneous experiences, pure energy that completes you instantly, that makes you whole.
You get exactly what you need, everything you were missing in one
spontaneous event. In a world where God is hidden, where permission
is in shadow, where there are no practices to expect or integrate the sacred, there is no vessel prepared for this experience. The rational mind
was not consulted upon entry into this dream-gate. It comes back with
a vengeance.

Remember when the Israelites crossed the Red Sea? This crossing
marked the fiftieth gate of consciousness, the high of highs. Three days
later King Amalek attacked. Amalek always attacks and sends us back

to our own Egypt. That's his job. An alcoholic wants recovery, but three days later he or she is drinking again. For a moment, recovery becomes the primary identity. Then, the flip. We become stuck in a one-or-the-other polarity. In romance, a numinous "we" momentarily becomes the primary polarity. All is wonderful. Then the flip. We return to our everyday rational selves, the drudgery, the suffering, the loneliness, the incompleteness. Maybe it was all an illusion. That's what the rationalists would like you to believe. Your experience was an illusion. Don't trust it, it will only lead you down the garden path. But our nature is to dream high. In the background of getting up in the morning, of our raison d'etre of everything we do, is a high dream. Faust asks Mephistopheles to show him his love. Mephistopheles paints a portrait in mid-air. Faust sees his love in this portrait, invisible to all but him. Then, as the real flesh-and-blood Gertrude walks by, you see Faust instantly take the image on the portrait and put it on Gertrude.

Does Gertrude participate in this? Yes. In this synchronicity, something in Gertrude flirts with Faust. But the essential truth is that Faust held his entire high dream, his experienced whole-making state—"love"—in the image of Gertrude rather than the flow of his own energy and the rhythm of his "love." That's how love is lost. That's how the High Dream becomes experienced outside oneself in the image of the other.

What happens when you live in that distortion? You find people, dramas, and behaviors that seek and fit the image of the magical other. You hunt for prey that fits the image. You pretend that your heart is involved, that you are concerned, that your essence is love. From the externalizing moment, you are eternally busy. Your mission is clarified. You know exactly what you want. You live the certainty you always hoped for, even if it must remain a secret for everyone else. The answer? Remember the Oedipus myth where Oedipus answers the riddle of the Sphinx and inherits the kingdom? The modern rational mind always has the answer. We can't help ourselves. We answer. The high dream is then captured, safely hidden in multiple layers of images, rituals, rules, and behaviors, rather than the essence energy: love, experience and completeness from within.

What real-life-people and activities do we seek out or fantasize? What images are magnets for our high dream? Those aspects of our shadow, whose archetypal forms mystify us, frustrate us, flirt with us, and drive us crazy, make the best bed-fellows, instigators of drama, tragedy, and fate. You can spend your lifetime looking for the perfect Mother or searching for the adequate Father because they are imprinted in you from birth, and they should be there because their impressions are. Or, you may be a lightning-rod chosen to express a shadow role, an energized figure or disavowed truth created by the field of your family and your fellow man, that you are best suited to express. You are compelled.

A metaphysical truth is you can't desire what you haven't lost. Those split-off, disavowed energies that drive the labyrinths of our complex behaviors, attitudes, and beliefs secretly hold the High Dream of nature's unadulterated archetype. Our shadows reveal the essence of our wholeness when these disparate worlds, figures, behaviors, and states are rejoined, included, added together, and embodied. After all, these are your energies.

Kit seems addicted to "bad boys." It doesn't start out that way. Thirty-five, beautiful, and established professionally, she attracts men of all education levels and colors. As soon as she meets them, they grow concerned—about her soul, about her future, about her. She is eminently concern-worthy. For her part, she sees their attractiveness and their seeming sensitivity. She is seduced by their engaging veneers only to be inevitably disappointed, betrayed, and devastated.

Overtly strong, opinionated, and very together, Kit identifies as a strong individual, a modern woman freed from the complexes that held her mother. Jung once responded to the idea that we don't have complexes, "The complexes have us." Everybody but Kit can see her dysfunctional behavior, its maladaptive pattern, its addictive repetition always leading to the same result. Kit can hire a coach or therapist to guide her to appropriate behavior, perception, and relationship. She can identify and interrupt her act-out once and for all. She can join the rest of society in functional and acceptable behavior. She can throw out the baby with the bathwater and be proud, except that the baby is the High Dream chased and reenacted through a drama of image, behavior, and repetition outside the person. Kit's essence Big "I" embodies love, desire, and permission.

Dry-drunk describes alcoholism that persists long after the person has had his or her last drink. Dry-drunks have never incorporated the high dream that alcohol supported. They are stuck in the misery of self-envy, the high dream in the background that will never be theirs to live. This high dream is the energy, state, and flow of life that is Kit's own Higher-Self nature. You might as well talk about a Martian invading your body—the rational mind can't conceive of reexperiencing and living this energy from within, even though it's right there. Remember the procession of the healing Holy Grail right in the Wounded King's own castle? Similarly, the High Dream is our healing chalice right there in our midst.

Our culture prescribes that Kit confess, repent, and see the error of her ways. But the stubborn persistence of Kit's repetitive behavior indicates a high dream. Disavowing the high dream is like living as a dry-drunk. Giving up these behaviors without accessing the high dream behind them restores the established dysfunctional order of suppressing the biggest part of your nature. No matter how socially successful your adaptation becomes, the misery of selling out, settling for crumbs, reverting to living your fate rather than your destiny, prevails. Don't fret. Fate will always lead you to the Self. While fate takes us to our inevitable devastation, it always brings us to the Self. Our natural path, individuation includes fate. Fate is our low-dark dream.

One way of accessing our High Dream is through our fate. In fact, that's how most of us do it, the scenic route. How does our fate become our destiny? It's our choice. Jung observed that when you amplify one pole of an experience, really bring it out, it becomes its opposite. The paradox of oneness of our world: Opposites add up. They are an invisible continuum. Their disparity and split is an illusion. There is a dance and flow that includes both sides, which is revealed when one of the sides is amplified. The experience of fate needs to be joined and accepted rather than avoided. Your high dream includes the low dream and vice versa. You find your dance of life through either your high or your low dream because they are both. Our shadow bonding patterns bring these two fixated worlds next to each other, but they remain experienced as one or the other. Either the high dream is around or the low dream is. No mercy, no incorporation or synthesis of these two extreme experiences to their Essence. Identified as one or the other, there is no awareness, no consciousness, no Big "I" that has permission or choice. No flow. The worlds remain parallel. Only at the point of conscious choice, to join the experience and pay attention to this experience, does our second layer of awareness kick in. There is actually somebody home inside us, a detached grown-up witness minding the store. Fixed in one pole or the other, you may be proud, but you're drunk.

What is Kit's High Dream? It's her sense of being okay, her own solidness, her strength, and her intactness. It's going back to the state she experienced every time she felt noticed, loved, and appreciated by the male figure who was supposed to be there for her. Is this a product of repeated longings for her unavailable and distant father? Is this an expression of her renegade, secret taking for herself? Is this the antidote to the precocious little girl who fixed and took care of her depressed mother? Is there a lost little girl who was never mirrored and loved? All these rational observations never touch the High Dream Essence that the reenactment with "bad boys" holds. Kit's own Big "I," embodying it and living through it. Being there for herself with it. Her own feeling of completeness. No longer attributed to others outside herself. Kit stops reenacting her devastating drama with "bad boys."

We must experience our shadow from within, reaccumulating these split-off energies, engaging with them, adding them up. Identifying with them, you'll find their natural place and flow in your body and life. This is the spiritual work of our time, for you to be YOU.

CHAPTER 8

Depression's Gift

For Jung, the middle years are seen as a metaphor of life, like the course of the sun. Rising in the morning, seeing the world as bright, discovering our significance, convinced that we can attain all that we wish. At the stroke of noon, the descent begins with the reversal of our dreams and values, so cherished in the morning. The sun, now in contradiction with itself, draws in its rays instead of emitting them. Light and warmth on the decline, in midlife or slightly thereafter, we face our mortality, a time of crisis and self-doubt. "What am I to do with the rest of my life? What is there to look forward to but old age, infirmity, and death?" Instead of looking forward, we look backward. Midlife is also the period of the highest rates of divorce, depression, and suicide. It can bring the choice to step out of time and flow with seemingly oppositional experiences instead of drowning in their contradiction.

Jung saw a positive side to all this: While the first half of life requires channeling our energies in a single-minded, specific direction, resulting in a "one-sided personality" not yet able to actualize the Self, our Big "I," he suggests that the crisis of midlife awakens this undiscovered Self, the remainder of one's life providing the very opportunity needed for its realization. Thus begins the real work of individuation, the process of bringing to conscious awareness the developmental process unfolding within us,

Depression joins the downward pull, the pull of gravity, the pull toward death, moving downward, backward in time, rather than forward and flying high. Why this instinct toward death?

Jack, a fifty-eight-year-old man, suffers from severe depression during the same period every year, the time around the anniversary of his father's suicide. He experiences his depression as a black hole, pulling him to commit suicide, and he's petrified of his impulse to do it. Jack has had access to the best in psychiatry and psychology. All of his doctors and mentors have supported him and urged him to live, but that doesn't seem to be Jack's direction, which is to die. Death is the ten-thousand pound gorilla at the background of depression.

WHY A DEATH EXPERIENCE?

Following are the paths that join to, and are congruent with, our essence, which is always there. The first path is death. A second path is war. The third path is the middle, or central, path. All three require leaving the safety of the established order and consciously participating in what's trying to occur. Why do we need to leave our small reality and embrace the intention of the bigger nature? Because, being unconscious, the inertia of our smaller direction always takes us to our physical destruction. Our eternal bigger part must guide us to our new reality, must help us transcend and combine all our worlds.

An equivalent of this can be found in the Old Testament: Instead of the quickest and most direct route to the Promised Land, which would have been traveling east along the Northern coast of Sinai, Moses went south (down) to the desert, into emptiness. Going down into emptiness takes you out of time and space. Traveling back in time, you find your indivisible essence. How do we take such a journey? Do we need to be a Moses? The answer is, "yes." This shamanic guide that navigates us through all kinds of contradictions and annihilations is not local to Moses; it resides in all of us. Awakened to our experience, our awareness welcomes the larger aspect of our self that transcends time and mortality.

How is this born? For most of us, our ally, guide, and higher Self is revealed in the ashes of our annihilation. The problem brings out our biggest nature. Moses's journey was the second Exodus. The first Exodus, along the quick route, resulted in the death of all, destroyed by their inevitable enemy. From that destruction, Moses emerged. Our problems and destructions reveal our own Big "I's." We are not reliant on others to be our guide.

Depression, reluctance, self-destruction, all join the pull of gravity, the pull toward death, the direction of going back in time, going downward, going backward not forward. Not flying high. Onward and upward take a back seat to going downward. Why this instinct toward death? Jung called this instinct a necessary rite of passage—symbolized in all the hero myths, man leaves home, goes through supreme ordeals, such as fighting a dragon, thus cutting away from the mother, to be reborn as a Self-determined man. As we've said, the three paths that return us to essence, death, war, and the middle path, require choosing death, its experience and ritual. Holidays like Good Friday and Yom Kippur are death experiences. They should be our own deep experience, rather than our relegating our personal experience of death to goats and the symbol of Christ, unless, of course, we understand fully that the goat and the Christ are us. We yearn for these experiences so that we can go back to our essence, so that we can start fresh and be guided by our bigger Self. We need to experience our own death and resurrection; otherwise it's fate that takes over.

This rite of passage, according to Jung, is innate—and so Jack would be steeped in this, whether conscious of it or not. He has both the capacity and the desire to experience death and be reborn. Nothing short of a conscious participation in a death rite will do. When Jack makes sacred space to imagine his own death, by suicide, he emerges from the darkness more alive than he has ever been. The pull to die is over, the trance broken.

Gary is thirty-three years old and miserable. He was always an outsider acting as if he fitted in, but about a year ago he gave up all pretense of fitting in and joining others. Having an extensive family, he continues to be invited to many functions, but he avoids them. "What's the use? I give up. I'm destined to be alone. I tried doing everything I've learned but nothing works. What I feel is sadness."

As a Christian, Gary believes in Jesus and understands that Christ is within. Knowing this, Gary found the idea of participating in his own death/resurrection ritual meaningful. Gary has bad knees and some early arthritis. He imagines that the stiffness in his knees takes over his whole body, and he dies. In a therapy session, Gary, lying face down, feels his life force ebb away from him as he goes into emptiness. Only his awareness remains. After a minute, he notices a sense of busyness all around. A lot of stuff is happening. A lot of traffic, light, and energy are all around, shooting by. Encouraged by the therapist, Gary makes motions with his hands depicting the energy all around him. Asked what special spot on earth that he knows has this energy, he looks down for a second and then says, "Kennedy Airport. That's the spot." Gary starts to imagine what it's like to be Kennedy airport, what it's like for him to be the spot of all this traffic and energy. He starts to move around, trying to walk in a couple of different directions and suddenly stops. Not moving, he stays perfectly still. Is he displaying an edge or resistance to continuing? No. Gary is perfectly fine. The essence is "stillness." Continuing with this new experience, Gary holds his stillness. He senses that stillness may be very useful. He notices its detachment. Unlike his daily walking-around identity, which he says, "always wants to get the hell out of here," stillness stays. It's present. It doesn't take things personally. "I'm calm." How to use this in everyday life? "I can be direct. I can stay and react to what is going on. I'm clear, not anxious or scared."

Gary's death experience brings the detached essence-awareness that transcends time and space and is there for him as guide and ally through his parallel and contradictory worlds. It is his own personal Moses. Gary can now react to others, connect to them, and not lose himself. No longer needing to run, he can "take in" and stay. He now has stillness; it is who he is. He died and was "reborn."

Does Gary's participation in his own death ritual have meaning for all of us? Yes. How? Participating in your own death, you find your essence. That is, we have a heavenly level where we can experience everything, the collision of our parallel worlds, the paths of all our possibilities as well as our death and resurrection. The moment of conscious choice of going into the experience instantly reflects the Big "I" essence dream behind our life. Jung said that the spark of your life comes from the darkest spot. Somewhere in midlife our one-sided personality becomes problematic—this includes depression, a darkness. But this can lead to the discovery of Self, where the process of individuation can begin—that process of bringing to conscious awareness the individual path unfolding within oneself.

Thus, through trauma there is the opportunity to become more conscious and to grow.

The paradox of existence is that light is in the background of the dark; that actually darkness was created: the light was always there. When we choose death, we travel back (downward) into our darkness and reconnect with the light of our own creation. The key is that it takes our own trust and choice to find what is going on meaningful, to not discard our symptoms, problems, pains, and tragedies as random events. We must learn not to marginalize our daily events, inconveniences, and subtle experiences appearing on the periphery of our awareness as irrational, distracting garbage to be discarded but, rather, understand that all of our nature seeks realization and inclusion. No one is a step-child.

Let's look at all the behaviors of everyday life that actually seek death: drinking to blackout, unrestricted sex, martyrdom, suicide, and giving up on life. How about drugs? Historically, the progression of substance abuse brings people to a bottom. A bottom is a death. There's a saying that everybody gets the message thirty seconds before they die, but it's not true. It takes death to get the message. Then, and only then, does the spark of life emerge. It takes going back to nothingness, to total blackness, to the unknown, to reexperience life. Denying life is a two-edged sword: A warrior gives up everything, all attachments. He has nothing to lose. He has already died. What does this have to do with addiction? Addicts imitate the warrior and act as if they have nothing to lose, denying the part of them that does. And, they make this denial their way of life. Nothing new ever happens in this cycle between not caring and caring too much. Until a bottom is experienced and a death lived through, there's no need to change or leave the certainty of the familiar, where one extreme or the other, not caring or caring too much, prevails.

All these experiences seem random and autonomous until somebody notices what is going on. Why notice? Jung distinguished neurotic suffering from real suffering. Neurotic suffering refers to the devil we know, the secret gain, control, and adequacy we know from our familiar and dependable repetitions, dramas, addictions, and fetishes, no matter how destructive their course. Real suffering is the feeling of pain. The drama of suffering versus real experienced devastation and pain. Feeling is the function that requires awareness—a partner, a witness, a second reality that is able to notice must be present. Pain brings this second reality. Without our special awareness, we eternally collide. This means that when something new and good happens, it inevitably collides with the old and bad. Something is always destroyed. It takes a Big "I" awareness to guide us to include our disparate worlds without destruction. Your path is health. Moving forward without awareness, unaware, health will collide with nonhealth and annihilate you. A one-sided identification with health will compel its opposite, nonhealth, to manifest. Only our Big "I" can bring these worlds together.

Many people equate awareness with intellectualism, cold detachment, and rational thinking. Lynn coveted these traits. Lynn always sought leadership positions, and she dreamed of going into politics and running for office. But, she found herself overwhelmed in large groups and forums, being obliged to take sides and at the same time being devastated by criticism, accusations of unfairness, and prejudice. Depressed about this, she wanted to give up her political aspirations. If she couldn't tolerate a local community meeting, how could she run for office? This caused even further depression. When asked how she felt in these groups, she said, "I want to die." Would it be worth it for her to experience her death? Yes. Lynn agreed to imagine dying in the middle of a group.

She lay down, closed her eyes, and imagined dying of mortification. For several minutes she lay still, and then she began reporting on the images and experiences that flirted with her. Initially describing emptiness, she first sees an animal in the distance, maybe a lion. She reports that she is on an African plain with many animals wandering to and fro. Encouraged to look around and see what really captures her attention, she first says, "A lion," but then she checks it out and realizes that that's not it. Looking around, she notices a tree, a big, solid, well-rooted tree that extends into the sky, bridging "heaven and earth." Remember Lynn's initial problem, being overwhelmed, wanting to die rather than stay in the group? What happens when Lynn's biggest nature is this tree? Lynn becomes this tree: tall, steady, rooted, solid, and complete unto itself. Lynn's eyes open wide, ready to see everything. What is the essence of this tree? "It stays right there." It witnesses everything. It has no invested agenda or result. It's neutral. It's not self-conscious. It's detached but present. "It will stay there no matter what happens." That's her leader. That's her guide. That's her martial artist. That's her shaman. This is the big part of us that can transcend our opposing worlds, our diversities, and bring them together. This is the part of ourselves that makes allies out of our perceived enemies. But when you face one of your allies, you need to bring more than your naïve good intentions. You need to be ready. It takes the guidance of your Big "I" not to be annihilated. Without this Big "I," your enemy-allies hunt you down and continue to do so because they're the bigger part of you pushing you to be whole.

"Love thy neighbor as thyself. I am God." One realization, that the neighbor is you, may be a revelation to some. Superficially, God simply knows best, so we should follow his rules. Rodney King asked, "Can't we all just get along?" Those are the words, but that isn't the process. The process says that you are both yourself and your neighbor. When your neighbor is the "other," God works. When you are confronted with this "other," you participate in the action and process that is present. In Taoism, Buddhism, and Hinduism, this is called "Tao," But it is also known in other religions and cultures as God, Shaman, Christ, the Force, and the Holy Ghost. Combining with the "other" brings a state of God, an indivisible essence. You become the "I" of the "I am God" when you embody your essence. This "I" transcends time, space, and mortality. The dream behind your birth, your nature, and your path of individuation is this Big "I."

Often, we're guided downward, toward death. The house we constructed, the provisional personality we've adopted, the beliefs we rely on, need to be destroyed. We're so identified with these forms that we actually think that their destruction is our destruction. The irony is that we must experience our own destruction to reexperience and realize the essence that is driving our life. Jung called this "Self." Depression and its downward pull take you there, to a path of silence and stillness. Silence is the means. Have you ever been caught in the swirl of a depression? Rootless, bottomless, endless. Sinking. Darkness. Is giving up an option? We must give up the drama to rejoin the process. The drama of giving up keeps us right there, making no changes, as this drama becomes the familiar and safe. Even the drama of self-harm and suicide is safer than participating in what's trying to happen. While people around you push you to "snap out of it," Jung would celebrate what is trying to come forth. Don't snap out of it. Snap into it.

Ted, thirty-eight, is married and is very unhappy. He says, "I'm always depressed and it's getting worse. I just don't know what to do with my life." He dreams: "I am with a woman that I don't know but realize that I love her. I sacrifice everything for her, like a martyr and then she is gone. I'm devastated."

You can imagine that the dream reflects Ted's actual experience with women, and it has. But why? In fact, Ted knows no other way than to fall into unrestricted devotion and responsibility for everything. And he repeats the pattern to the point where his own desire and path are totally forsaken. He doesn't know any other lifestyle. Jung would call the female in the dream the "anima" which in Greek means "soul." The "anima" is the feminine, associated with feeling, Ted's feeling function. The dream reflects that Ted's feelings have him, not that he has feelings. Jung makes a crucial distinction between feeling and emotion. Feeling is an earthly, rational, evaluating function. Emotions are the raw, unharnessed archetypal forces of nature and as such provoke biochemical responses in the body. The basic distinction is that real change requires emotion.

Ted's female represents "the other," and Ted is entranced, mesmerized, awed. Caught in a tidal wave, he has no awareness. Completely submerged to her mood, her need, and his fear of her abandoning him, he is desperate. Nothing else exists. The feeling is the fact. There is no Ted. The drama of enslavement and martyrdom to the image of the woman secretly holds the feeling essence. There is the female archetype and the female complex. The former contains the soul, the love, feelings, passion, the body, earth, as indivisible essences. The complex is the fragmented version. In Ted, it is the drama of love, rescue, martyrdom, and loss that he reenacts.

With no awareness, Ted eternally repeats this drama, constantly reliving his own destruction. The dream shows that there are two parts of Ted: that Ted is potentially the sum of both himself and the woman. How does he realize this? Basically, what we need is a Big "I" to notice our direction, to guide us out of our inevitable destruction, toward the inclusion of all our worlds. The paradox of inclusion is that we need our biggest "I" to find our biggest "I." How? Start by noticing: Notice your self as if you're outside yourself. Notice what you notice, what's "flirting" for you. Is it an image? A body sensation? A movement? A fantasy? A craving? An object? An irrational thought? Upon noticing and staying, you've now entered the doorway to your eternal "You." Check your rational mind. What is it doing? Are you thinking your way out of this? Are you putting it down? Did you notice something, then give up and explain it away as a distraction or a figment of your imagination? Can you sense the difference between noticing something or just rationally thinking about it? Can you notice yourself rationally thinking? A "noticer" is part of what's trying to happen. Without a "noticer," we can never join the dream. We remain unconscious and stuck in the fragmented version of our essence. Our worlds remain disparate, and we have no guide to preclude our inevitable destruction. No wonder we're depressed.

Back to Ted. His pattern may be so embedded that he may never have actually felt the pain of his enslavement. Pain inspires notice. Pain provokes witness. Without a witness, Ted is not there yet. His therapist hopes that Ted moves from his pain to becoming the "noticer," not merely the one who feels pain. Without a witness, we're drunk and carry no responsibility. The drama has its own inertia. No choice is even necessary. Our detached witness is ultimately a warrior, a martial artist: God, King, Queen, Prophet, Healer, Yogi, Shaman, Mother, Father are all names for our Big "I," our indivisible essence attribute and realization. It is our second awareness, the guide we need to transcend our inevitable destruction and include all our worlds. The ally we yearn for. Without the High Self, we're all alone. What happens when you're all alone is that you're really not here. But you're always busy; avoiding fate is a full-time job.

Take Fred, for instance, who says he's isolated. He says he doesn't really need anyone and says it with pride. Fred has sniffed heroin daily for the last twenty years. He is now forty-two. Complaining of misery and putting down his habit is one side of the story. When Fred tells the story of his first high on heroin, he becomes fluid, energized, and enlivened. He describes an unexpected, spontaneous warmth and quietness that he always craved but never experienced. He feels perfect. No guilt, no anxiety, no aloneness. "Completely OK myself, I don't need anybody." Instant completeness. The best lies are hooked on truth. Fred tells himself that it's the heroin that makes him complete. Big secret: Fred is the heroin. Bigger secret: Heroin is the dream that's trying to happen. Biggest secret: The heroin dream incarnated is Fred's Big "I." That's where Fred's action is. That's where God is hiding. That's Fred's biggest ally. Yes, heroin. Not the drug.

In Fred, "OKness" looks like heroin. It's natural that heroin appears in his dream because its image embodies Fred's natural endowment of "OKness." The feeling, the energy, not the substance. That is the choice that the dream image brings: to feel this from within versus to inhale or inject an outside substance.

Imagine our dilemma: It is easy to attribute our power and completeness outside ourselves. Why is completeness so terrifying? Because without a guide, the initial whole-making experience traumatizes. When we do not enter these experiences with our guide, we remain without permission and feel we've committed a theft; we've stolen completeness that we haven't earned or deserved. We then revert to depression and guilt of our shame-based identity, the incomplete one, the one that needs the heroin to be whole. Fred is potentially the sum of his two parts. Without awareness, these two worlds will collide and annihilate each other, rather than find the dance between the two.

Every day, Fred wakes up nervous, burdened, and guilty. For as long as he can remember, something has been wrong. Shy, inadequate, with difficulty concentrating, Fred hears a constant drumbeat of self-criticism. But when taking heroin, suddenly everything was right, just the way it should be: no criticism, no guilt. "I can take what I want. And I want heroin. And I'll do whatever I have to, to get it." Upon entering treatment Fred started dreaming about heroin. Heroin is his recurring dream. What is the heroin in the dream? It's his state of warmth, completeness, and permission to take. It's his sense of being "okay" and his sense of adequacy. It's the natural rhythm, flow, and confidence of his larger nature. As a dream, this large part of Fred's nature is experienced outside himself. Fred remains in the self-reinforced truth that there is something wrong, that he's defective, that he must live a life in envy of all the others who "have it." As his completeness is nonlocal, he sees it in heroin, but never in himself. The reexperience of completeness that heroin brings is like something stolen in the night. He didn't earn it or consciously participate in its unfolding. Our rational mind colludes with our small self and does not experience the dream from within that is unfolding. It objectifies the dream and calls it heroin.

Even after twenty years, long after, heroin powder does not make him high anymore. The dream remains. The missing aspect in most conventional treatment of behavior is not going back to the dream behind the original behavior. The dream is akin to returning to the spirit—the essence-archetype behind the complex of destructive behaviors and beliefs. Behind these behaviors, beliefs, moods, attitudes, and patterns drives an archetypal essence, the very essence that makes you whole. Unfolded, embodied, and identified with, this essence transcends into your Big "I," lands on earth and notices our own suffering. Hand-in-hand with our "something's wrong" self, we become both guide and guided. We transcend our fated destructions. The third path: "I give you blessings and curses, choose life"; this third path is the sum inclusion of the polarized fragments of the first two. Blessings *plus* curses equals "Choose life." Blessings *or* curses, choosing only one or the other, equals inevitable destruction.

Fred remembers his first high as if it happened yesterday, his warmth, his confidence, his aliveness, his relaxation. He says that the energy and the confidence that he feels when he's on heroin remind him of being like Martin Luther King, who was able to use his calmness and confidence to "move the world." Fred demonstrates this calmness, this confidence, and this "move the world" leadership with his hands. Encouraged, he begins to walk with the energy of this movement. The walk is slow. Fred is relaxed, confident, and completely awake. In his Martin Luther King state he walks around, slowly, in his ever-present cadence. His therapist begins to act his "something's wrong, inadequate" world. Taking on this inadequate role, the therapist acts lost and unaware of Big Fred's presence or existence. Simulating little Fred, the therapist acts the drudgery, inevitability, and loneliness of life. Continuing the separate walks, suddenly, their paths cross, wherein Martin (Fred) responds immediately. He starts to help the therapist, guiding, helping, never leaving. He is totally there. They walk around together. Martin makes life easy. The burden is lifted. And then they switch. The therapist becomes Martin and Fred becomes "something's wrong." The experience is duplicated.

Fred gave up heroin. Learning to listen, to notice, to care about himself, Fred started to live in his big "I" essence that transcended his desire for heroin.

CHAPTER 9

Shadow Homeopathy

In his middle years Jung went through a midlife crisis. It was during this time that he discovered alchemy. The alchemists touched his experiences, along with his understanding of the unconscious. Although alchemists were dismissed as a crude part of chemistry, Jung believed that, in their efforts to "cook" base metal into gold, alchemists were engaged in a process of psychic transformation—that alchemy is a metaphor for individuation. An elaborate discipline based upon the psychological phenomenon of projection, Jung saw alchemical transformation as a model of transference and countertransference occurring between analyst and patient, guideposts of the course of analytic relationship. Jung's discovery of alchemical symbols in dreams confirmed the validity of his insights about the therapeutic relationship as a field for individuation. He now conceived of analysis more as a means to personal growth than as a technique for treating mental disorder.

Symptom formation is itself a product of the individuation process; symptoms are organized by higher intent and are a creative act, a function of the psyche's imperative to grow and develop. Neurosis is a form of adaptation, if an "inferior" one, of a potentially healthy organism responding to the demands of life; what is going on in the head is also going on in the body, and the process behind both is wholeness. Self-awareness comes from confronting problems, wrestling with them to get their energy, bringing the encounter with the Self that makes us whole. The Big "I," the magical "third," that results from this encounter has the capacity to lessen or even eliminate symptoms when their energy and vitality have been incorporated and lived.

Our cases are presented with this in mind. Symptom formation is a creative act: a soul struggling to find fulfillment, an opportunity to become conscious and to grow. Like Jung, homeopathic medicine is different from allopathic medicine in that it recognizes that what is happening is a process seeking completion. Allopathic medicine and rational thinking see symptom phenomena as a problem with a disease locus that needs to be removed or subdued, not joined. In homeopathy, the Law of Similars prevails. Like cures like, not by removing or destroying the problem but by trusting, supporting, and amplifying what is happening in the body, in the psyche, in the outer world.

LIKE CURES LIKE

The fact that a symptom like nausea can paradoxically be cured with minute amounts of a substance that induces nausea is antithetical to the rational mind. But this is exactly the knowledge that ancient wisdom bestows. The Kosher laws are predicated on similar wisdom. If the problem or contamination is caused by heat, it takes heat, not cold, to restore something to its essence. Jung uses the Alchemical Model and the metaphor of fire and cooking to understand this phenomenon and find its equivalent in the human psyche in its search for the Self, which parallels nature's processes. Jung's Self transcends the ego and inheres the age-old capacities of the species, its goal being the blueprint for human existence within the context of the life of the person, particularly in the inner life of the soul — or the God within. Exactly what we need is already there. At the center of a symptom or a complex is the archetype around which it is organized. In terms of homeopathy, a homeopathic intervention would embrace the problem or symptom, follow its direction, and finally, join its energy, since the symptom, no matter how disturbing, always stores the archetypal essence that is trying to happen. Like cures like because it amplifies the archetypal Self energy that is at the Center of the symptom, awakening its inclusion in the flow of life, which Jung symbolized as the restoration of the Self-ego axis.

A homeopathic intervention in such cases provokes transformation through embracing the problem or symptom, following its direction, and finally joining it, because the symptom, no matter how disturbing, always stores the archetypal essence that is trying to happen.

Everything in the universe seeks reflection. The most basic instinct is reflection. Without reflection, we get stuck too early in an irresolvable image, something like the sound of one hand clapping. The reflection should be there. We expect it. Early psyche needs constant reflection to validate its existence, to experience itself. While most psychologists maintained that children were passive recipients of maternal care, Jung maintained that children actively participate in the formation of their relationship with the world, that we bring with us an innate psychic structure enabling us to have this experience. The expectation of the responding other occurs with the first breath. A failed response wounds and shames immediately. And shame commonly entails shut down; lacking a mirror, we shut down our imprinted essence. Shame creates reality. Our first responders become our great determiners. Do we get mirrored and supported for who we are? Or do we survive and hide our essence? Do we mirror the merciful side of God or the punitive?

When you are not mirrored to the level of your imprinted expectations and endowment, you are bad. Something is wrong with you. One early experience is envy, where we project our good stuff on the other. We experiment with our own good stuff, and when the other does not reflect back, we get hit with two barrels. The other remains the possessor of the very attributes that we invited to be reflected. Being bad, being defective, is bad enough. Now the other has it and won't give it to you. There is vengeance for ruining everything, and the paranoid-making burden of hiding this dangerous, vengeful truth, in the service of your survival.

GAINING PERMISSION

Whether in the first day, the first year, or the first decade of life, permission to experiment, permission for desire, permission for love, permission for acceptance, permission to receive takes second place to survival. To survive, we accumulate a primary identity that disavows those aspects of our personality, desire, and energy that seem dangerous to us. We think that we know ourselves and that we exercise a semblance of control, except for that unrelenting agenda just beneath the surface of daily life that involuntarily takes us back to the scene of the crime, the scene of the expected but denied reflection repeated over and over. New faces and new circumstances; same problem.

Why do these repetitions have such a hold on us? Why does a mother- or father-driven complex or role hold such power? Because the unmirrored essence is held in these images, the archetypal essence, attribute, desire, expression that completes the person and restores them to the imprinted natural path of their true nature before the "crime." For Jung, in order for the infant to receive what needs to be, the mother, the caretaking person, needs to show behaviors and personal characteristics sufficiently similar to the built-in structure of the maternal archetype for the child to perceive her and experience her as "mother." It is then, as the relationship develops, that this becomes active in the personal psyche of the child: through similarity, the mother's with the infant's internal mother image, like cures like, beginning at birth.

Coaching and behavioral techniques are sometimes useful strategies to help overcome problems, but they do not retrieve the essence held in shadow that the ongoing complex is trying to restore. There are two perspectives for understanding shadow. From the point of view of the essence, archetypal energy going into shadow is a judgment. From the point of view that the shadow holds the archetype's life essence for redemption, it is mercy.

Jacqueline was entering adolescence at the start of World War II. Today, she complains of chronic pain and inflammation in her left shoulder. She says that her main life problem is how hard things have always been for her, how much she has had to rush and put herself second and that she just doesn't have the energy anymore. She says resentfully, "Something's got to give." She describes the pain in her left shoulder as something constantly poking.

Initially, she returns to describing how bad the pain feels to her, but the key is to return to what "it," the pain, is doing, not how she feels about it. She shows a poking motion with her right hand and demonstrates the energy that is victimizing her left shoulder. Encouraged, she makes the pain now on my arm, her poking sharp, firm, and constant. Amplifying the poking movements with even more emphasis, suddenly

Jacqueline exclaims: "I see myself carrying my mother to the bomb shelter during the war. I'm eleven. As soon as the bombs started, she fainted. All her weight is on me, as if she's dead. I can't tell if she is dead. That's how I feel, as if her weight is on me."

Let's backtrack: when Jacqueline complains of a symptom she is describing something unknown from her day-to-day normal reality. What makes it a symptom is her sense of control, or lack of it, an experience of not being in control that falls outside the boundaries of Jacqueline's familiarity and identity. The body stores, holds, and keeps intact Jacqueline's essence that was disowned, held, stolen by the image of her mother. How does the energy of Jacqueline's symptom contain Jacqueline's essence? When Jacqueline begins to move like the energy and catch its intent, she sees the image of the mother and experiences the dead weight of her mother's "feebleness." Fixed in this experience and obligation, there is nothing in life for Jacqueline. Long after her actual mother's death, she seems stuck in this spell forever, stuck carrying dead weight. Ironically, the dead victimizing weight contains Jacqueline's essence energy in shadow form. What is the natural archetypal endowment hiding in plain sight of this fixed and traumatic image of long ago? Ironically, it's the weight. Being the weight, using her own natural weight, its gravity and inertia, leaning into her tasks with her weight, pushing forward with all her weight. This is so natural. This is what happens when Jacqueline becomes like the weight. Movement is easy and flowing. Rather than artificially pushing, forcing, and then giving up, she uses her weight. It's easy. What is Jacqueline's central essence experience of her weight? "It's my sturdiness."

Her whole life Jacqueline experienced a daily attack of the burden of the weight she had to carry—a constant ghost experienced in the body, so familiar it was hardly noticed. Now, with less subtlety, her shoulder symptom is expressing the same energy. Joining the process returns Jacqueline to the clear image and experience of carrying the dead weight of the mother. This image fixed on a point where Jacqueline's nature, "sturdiness," was virtually stolen by the image of the mother. Jacqueline's attributes—using her weight, expressing from the weight of her weight, leaning in without hesitating, keeping going naturally with the inertia of her weight—are captured in the word that embodies the essence of her attributes, "sturdiness, this is my sturdiness"—a "sturdiness" that is its own attribute and higher level of awareness, Jacqueline's ally—a Big Jacqueline, a sturdy individual separate from her feeble mother. Living from her own "sturdiness," Jacqueline's energy and vitality are resurrected. No longer stuck in the trance of never getting and always carrying the other's burden, with sturdiness, Jacqueline has started to care for herself and identify activities and participations based on her own desire and need. She is saying "no" and carving out time for herself, naturally, without guilt or vengeance, rather than being eternally consumed by the needs and demands of others before her own.

Helen has chronic asthma and complains of difficulty in breathing and being desperate for breath during asthma attacks at least twice a day. When asked to describe what the asthma is doing, she speaks about her shortness of breath and her sense of being choked. Speaking from her normal day-to-day identity as someone who feels victimized by the attacks and who feels out of control, Helen identifies as the choked one, and now demonstrating what the choking feels like by firmly squeezing her therapist's hand, Helen smiles. She enjoys her strength. While sustaining the squeeze, she suddenly says, "Oh! This is my father, controlling. I don't want to do that. It's bad." At the edge of Helen joining and sustaining this energy is the image of a judgmental father, judging, ruling, controlling. You can sense that part of Helen's essence. Strength and steadiness have been stuck in the image of a controlling father, a father-complex, an image that holds Helen's own vital essence. A parallel process exists between the mind, the body, and all our worlds. Like the "Rainmaker," that also means that Tao, natural order consciously restored in one of our worlds is synchronized with all our worlds.

The problem is asthma and the ghost of her father complex where Helen continues to hide her own strength and project her enjoyment and steadiness onto others. Like many of us, Helen lives out an aspect of this essence in split and compartmentalized form. She is strong, rock-steady, and happy for others, but not herself. She chooses partners and friends who need her strength and who receive it. In this manner, Helen's Big "I" essence stays outside herself in sacrifice and service to others, remaining with the lack of permission for her to live for herself and be happy. Now, by joining her strength, rock-steadiness, and joy at being strong and using it in the world, Helen's need for her asthma medication dwindled. The energy behind the asthma was the solution for Helen's rejoining the flow of her nature, path and Self-realization.

Robert was scheduled for surgery for his carpal tunnel syndrome. The inflammation around his left elbow and forearm was constant and debilitating. Robert relies on his computer for work, and he was now able to type only with his right hand. He had seen two specialists and both recommended surgery. Robert is a kind gentleman who is impeccable about his sobriety. He works hard on himself and his recovery from alcoholism. He treats people well and with respect. Professionally, he always goes the extra mile and is often victimized by aggressive, self-serving individuals who take advantage of his extensive preparation and footwork. They work off the information he develops. They steal his clients.

When describing his pain, Robert called it "a fire, raging." To show the energy of the raging fire, Robert forcefully raised himself, then bounded out of the chair. He repeated this cycle of forcefully bounding out of the chair, then slowed it down. What is the attitude behind the bounding? "It's ruthless."

Robert tells a story about ruthlessness. "There was a ruthless man who never hesitated. He never doubted what his next action would be. He was there to get his. There were no doubts. He doesn't need permission. His job is to take. If he has to bullshit, he does it intentionally. Let the others have second thoughts. He is here to take everything he can get."

Robert started to walk using this attitude and energy. He was tall, solid, and forceful. No pity. Very awake, alive, and mindful of his own needs. This vital "Me" aspect had somehow gotten lost in the rules of his recovery from alcoholism, in the spiritual correctness of being spiritual. Nature, however, does not let Robert off the hook of his own wholeness. The attacks by the aggressive self-serving individuals and the carpal tunnel syndrome contain the storehouse of Robert's disavowed and projected energies. How ironic that the emergence of these shadows and the "Me" essence they secretly contain are identical to the high Robert first got from Scotch. Robert grew up without permission to take for himself. First, alcohol supported this "I"; now, symptomatically, the aggressive, self-serving individuals and the carpal tunnel syndrome do. These are the disturbing shadow figures that awaken Robert. The process of Robert's wholeness and Big "I" continues. There is no diminution of a process, just direction, form, and awareness. Upon Robert's telling the story and walk of ruthlessness, the pain disappeared and to this day has never returned.

Martin is a fifty-four-year-old male who has had strabismus (double vision) since a childhood football accident at age nine. He has adjusted to this symptom so well he hardly notices it anymore. He has adapted perfectly. His mastery of the disturbance of seeing two images at once is so complete, he takes it for granted.

Martin complains of trouble getting things finished. A lifelong problem, Martin says he is chronically frustrated. He gets inspired and starts something but then gets frustrated and gives up because it's too difficult. Does the energy behind the double vision reveal anything about the problem of getting things finished? The incongruity in this symptom is its nondisturbance. The instant adaptation that Martin makes moment-to-moment seems to hold a powerful essence, but what really happens is so automatic and so fast that its essence is no longer identified. The capacity and rhythm that the symptom and adaptation bring remain compartmentalized in the double vision syndrome, literally hiding in plain sight on the periphery of Martin's conscious awareness.

When Martin slows down his automatic method of seeing and hones in on an image, he notices that one eye instantly shuts down. He is only aware of seeing out of one eye at a time, the eye he is using, and that seeing eye is focused and concentrated. Then it's the right eye's turn. In a blink, the seeing eye shuts down and now the right eye hones in and focuses sharply. And that seeing eye is now focused and concentrated. Going from vision task to vision task second by second, you catch an amazing rhythm, which Martin demonstrates with his hands. First, the awakening of the left eye by holding the left hand up with a fist. This aspect has strength. Concentration occurs. Correspondingly, the right eye shuts off, the right fist is down. Then, it's the right eye's turn to see, focus, concentrate. The right fist goes up and the left fist goes down, indicating the left eye shut down. There is a one-at-a-time rhythm with a space for concentration between each change and focus. The rhythm feels powerful, not rushed. Meaningful. Present. Concentrated. Focused. It is natural and takes no conscious effort.

Remember Martin's problem with getting things finished and staying focused? That one-at-a-time rhythm has been a lifesaver. Reading has now become effortless. Tasks that were daunting are now easily done. Martin's house is clean and in order. The mess is gone. Now that Martin lives from his slower, one-at-a-time rhythm he has found time for fun, joy, and relationship.

The symptom, unfolded, carries exactly the missing rhythm for concentration and completion with no tiredness that the problem requires. Imagine making a practice of taking all body symptoms and experiences seriously and treating them not as our life-burden but as our spiritual guides. Our dreams continue in the body. All history is stored. Disown an aspect of your life-force, go unconscious, don't worry. The dream continues. There is no diminution of process, only of direction, form, and consciousness.

Rick is a thirty-year-old man who has trouble socially. While he experiences his peers as superficial, he envies their ability to engage, socialize, and meet girls. He sits on the sidelines in social situations. He dreams that he is at a social gathering and that a girl in very high spike heels is attempting to kick him in the chest. He stands there and absorbs the kick. The kick has no impact. Rick is happy and proud. He feels good.

Conventional psychology might see this image as a picture of the prevailing neurosis that prevents Rick from engagement, the gratifying experience of not being impacted by the attack of the female. A mastery over the feminine, a young, sexual, seductive female as indicated by the spike heel. Does she remind him of his mother? Is there enmeshment with the mother? Is Rick stuck between an irreconcilable desire versus a taboo around a young woman that duplicates something of mom? Is Rick's sideline behavior secretly gratifying? All these may be true, but the real question is: who orchestrated this dream and why? What is nature trying to unfold? Is the dream just trying to make conscious what is secretly driving Rick's behavior or is there more? Note the powerful, numinous experience of Rick feeling good, feeling proud, being in control.

Entering the dream experience at the point of numinosity, Rick goes back to the moment of receiving the blow, of its having no impact and feeling good. Embracing the physical posture of receiving the blow, feeling his muscles and his skeletal structure and concentrating on his chest, Rick starts to walk with this attitude and posture. Encouraged by the therapist, Rick makes a movement with his hands that represents this energy, an outward thrust. Staying with this movement and then repeating it, Rick suddenly realizes, "It's a shield, my shield of detachment and protection."

Now, shields are a double-edged sword. Shields can be used to hide, but the essence shield that Rick experienced is for engagement. With the shield, Rick knows awareness. Using his shield, Rick knows detachment. The essence shield, the visceral sense of it and awareness of it, breaks the spell. Engagement is possible. Interaction is possible. Participation is manageable. Real desire restores. These visceral protectors are powerful Essences in our time and carry nature's permission, acceptance, and alliance.

A professional analyst is very disturbed by one of her clients. Even though the sessions are mostly on the phone, she dreads speaking to her. The client, a fortyish female professional, is unrelentingly intrusive and has no boundaries. You can bet that whenever an individual has such a powerful effect on you, negative or positive, there is shadow in you flirting for your attention. The therapist experiences the intrusion as "crawly bugs that swarm up my arms and then get into my clothes."

Though initially reluctant, the therapist agrees to demonstrate the energy of her client's intrusion. She uses all ten fingers as the bugs to convey the invasion of crawly bugs. Encouraged, the therapist now becomes those crawly bugs moving closer and threatening. Then she suddenly closes her eyes and sees a vision: A fence and gate. No fence, no gate, constant intrusion. No life. No permission. Only intrusion. The therapist's major complaint in life: "Everybody wants to suck me dry. I don't have time for anything." The fence and gate brings an "I," a sense of self, a permission to make a life, a Me.

Imagine a partnership with a person who does not have a fence or gate, where everything is intrusive. Imagine being the chosen recipient of the other pole, the unconscious intrusion when it hits. Imagine being a therapist who instills permission for life in and through others but doesn't have it for herself. Imagine in daily life how this invites the very intrusiveness that is needed to be whole. So with the fence/gate essence (both of which can be opened or shut) comes awareness, choice, and permission. The very attribute the therapist analyst hates, the very energy she despises in the other, completes her and gives her a life.

Knowing her fence and gate and living viscerally from its energy brings a sense of protection. No longer "naked" to the inevitable intrusion of others, this therapist now brings awareness and detachment to her practice. From her new vantage that embodies fence and gate, that provides adequate distance and detachment, this therapist can feel herself for the first time. She has an unenmeshed "me," no longer in the trauma of her unprotected, helpless, and all alone nakedness.

And with a "me" comes a "we." Not a "me" with a vengeance. Not a narcissistic "me," but a natural and distinct "me," with permission and acceptance for oneself, without guilt or self-consciousness to receive and to give. No longer feeling that everybody wants to suck her dry and that she has no time for anything, the therapist has learned to take time, have fun, laugh. No longer seeing her clients as the problem that needs fixing, she gives them permission to be who they are. It's contagious. In order to have a "we," you need a "me" first. The paradox of relationship is that a conscious "me" comes first. And that "me" often lives in shadow, in the image and experience of a very disturbing person, symptom, or addiction unrelentingly pushing to be included.

CHAPTER 10

Dark Angels

Jung felt the "shadow" (dark angel) to be a term for the disowned subpersonality—saying that there was something "shady" about it, dark, hidden away in the unconscious. However disavowed, unwanted, and threatening to society and the sense of control of the individual, the shadow persists as a powerful dynamic; we take it wherever we go, our dark companion. While much of the time we try to ignore it, it reminds us of its presence, in dreams, symptoms, and recapitulated events that bring this unconscious presence to our doorstep. Jung regarded this shadow as a cluster of traits, including that of the enemy, the most deadly, but also "gold." How does this hidden identity come about? Jung attributed it to two sources: cultural indoctrination, what we have been taught about out-groups, those hostile to one's in-group, and the concept of evil in our culture, such as Satan, the Devil, Hell. This shadow possesses the qualities opposite to those of our persona, compensating for its superficial pretensions, a way of balancing our provisional, false personality. Thus, it is both dark and an angel because it contains our secret light, energy, traits, and desires.

How do we know a dark angel when we see one? Why do we need messengers from heaven that entice us to participate in everything forbidden? Why do we need instigation and energy from outside ourselves just to get through the day? Why does our place and our role in society become such hard work? Isn't our own instinctual nature and wisdom enough? Why do some cultures accentuate feeling while others stress cold intellect? Why are the values of the heroin addicts of today so different from the heroin addicts of thirty years ago?

Fifty years ago, no addict worth his salt would think of living under the roof of his/her parents. Heroin addicts made sure they had their own place. Independence was paramount. It may have been an illusion, but the heroin cult, mores, tradition, and apprenticeship supported a rite of passage of personal truth and allegiance to that truth. Sacrifice, hard work, and devotion were required. Heroin was something worth fighting for, something worth suffering for, something that separated them from their contemporaries who glorified suburban sameness and fitting in, no risk.

These attributes of addiction arose in the midst of a postwar era that was materialistic, absent of conflict, lacking in things worth dying for. No risk necessary. You can trust and give yourself over to the authority. The addictions of the time supported the disavowed reality. Authority is inherently evil, don't trust it. Take care of yourself. Trust your experience. Don't fall into lock-step with everyone else. The suckers that settle for a few dollars—is this all there is? It can't be. It's not that conflict did not exist. Underneath the surface of suburban tranquility and the absence of diversity, racial conflict simmered and wars were fought. Remember how the rugged individual cowboy in the Old West became popular against a backdrop of citizens who lived in the certainty of their sense of control? That was heroin fifty years ago: a compensation for the absence of individuality and heroism.

The Dr. Jekylls of that time were serious, worshiped money, didn't take risks. The system will provide. Stay within the norms. Be successful. Be polite. Don't rock the boat and you'll be able to earn everything you need.

Mr. Hyde insists on more. Give me something to live for, fight for. That's what makes life really worth living. If it's worthwhile, I'll suffer gladly. I'll give everything. I don't care about your rules or myself. You're a coward. I'll do what I want even if it kills me. I don't need anyone or anything. I take what I need with no apology and no guilt.

Today's addicts follow the crowd, they're a lightning rod for the entitlement of our times. They show no devotion, no responsibility, no struggle, no fire. They take the easy way out every time, they whine, complain, act depressed. Rather than going against societal norms, they show a mastery of the prevailing culture, where safety is king. Unlike their predecessors, their behaviors and repetitions support Dr. Jekyll, not Mr. Hyde. No gadfly in this bunch. Safety is king. No experimentation, just sure things. People who abuse heroin, cocaine, marijuana, cannabis, gambling, sex, prescriptions, are still dying, primarily from the peripheral activities and consequences of their activities, not the addiction itself. Addictions used to burn through people when they supported the unconscious shadow, the Mr. Hyde side of the equation. One addiction that seems to burn through people today is anorexia, bulimia, and its combinations. Rooted in ideals of perfection and distortion of mortal reality, these behaviors parallel the cause greater than one's self, a calling and total devotion to a spirit or ideal that the addictions of forty years ago manifested.

What are some of the behaviors, philosophies, and addictions of today that support the unconscious shadow, Mr. Hyde? Here is our list:

- The terrorist-martyr of our day
- Tyrannical certainty: religious, spiritual, political, and cultural
- Gossip, slander, and accusation
- War, struggle, fighting, loyalty
- Depth, seriousness, real depression, humility, willingness to die

We can see why the old-time heroin addict would say: "I wouldn't want to use with this heroin bunch." The addictions of our time reflect the split in us, the Jekyll-Hyde polarity split. Jekyll represents all that is civilized, socialized. Hyde represents everything else, good and bad. Jekyll is the good boy or girl, responsible, controlled, rational, civilized, enslaved by the status quo; Jeckyll is a lifeless, passionless slave, scared and unfulfilled, who must serve others before him. Hyde is unrestricted, alive; Hyde feels no guilt, takes with a vengeance, and believes death is irrelevant.

The problem with the Jekyll and Hyde story is they stay split. They never have it out, they never even meet each other. They flip from one to the other. Ancient wisdom says that the enemy is your ally, one you must wrestle to the ground in order to get its energy. Every addiction, problem, or symptom brings your ally to your doorstep. Its appearance, its notice, its disturbance is organized by higher intent and holds your secret essence. The inception of addiction is an actual experience of instant wholeness. That first high cannot be tolerated.

Remember Adam's experience in the Garden of Eden. He had every-thing he needed—a natural, effortless instant connection to the entire universe. It was so good he went to sleep. We cannot tolerate our Gar-den of Eden without awareness. The process of descending from the Greeks' Dionysius ecstasy to the Roman version, Bacchus the drunk. Drunkenness is the direction of sleep, death, unconsciousness, where there is no feeling, no tension, no awareness, no suffering, no desire, no work.

Why do people feel perfect drinking three beers and then drink fifteen? The perfect state of the three beers is actually disturbing. It feels like an experience outside the self, one that is unearned, undeserved, something for nothing. The rational mind, that is the ego, can't take the spontaneous experience that is out of its control. Invaded by energy, feeling, insight, and desire not willed, entering a gate of feeling exactly how you always knew you could feel, for once with no permission necessary and no hovering guilt, you are exactly where and how you want to be. This experience, no matter how transient, becomes the high dream, the rich archetypal experi-ence waiting for realization. From the moment of that first high experience, the dream is in place and becomes the determiner of your identity, your pain, your pleasure, and your esteem. You relate and measure yourself by where you stand vis-à-vis this dream. From the point of the first high, the polarity is embedded. The high dream holds one pole, and the other pole is in the ordinary self: diminished, scared, miserable, and stuck in envy of their own completeness in others. This pair is exemplified in the biblical story of the twin brothers Jacob and Esau. We all evolve into twins. It was Jacob who understood that his problem was not his brother but himself. Like Jacob, it is vital to see our camps divided.

Those who do not wrestle with themselves never integrate the es-sence vitality dream of their addiction. They stay stuck in the same po-larity, flipping from one extreme to the other. In this way, they perpetu-ate the status quo and never integrate or experience the dance, rhythm, or energy between the two extreme poles. Very often people who are ashamed of their behavior feel its consequences make a commitment to being "good." Being "good" is just as one-sided as being "bad." In fact, being "good" is another form of the addiction. Being "good" gets tiring. The flip to the other pole is a sure thing. Addiction means being stuck in one of the poles of this polarity.

Awareness requires holding the tension of these opposites and accepting their contradiction. Carlos Castaneda says, "When you encounter a lion, you better have more than your farts to protect you." Your first high, your ecstatic experience, is your lion. But there is no witness. You did not consult your ordinary, rational mind to participate in this experience. You jumped over the edge of ordinary identity without permission.

Once over, permission was no longer needed. Worry and guilt disappeared. But the rational mind fights back and retakes the day. No one can tolerate this ecstatic experience without a witness, without a mirror, without a vessel of permission. Internalized, forbidden, and not mirrored, the high dream gets reflected and objectified outside the self through an addiction to forms, behaviors, and imitations that mimic rather than live the high dream experience. These are the behaviors of addiction, compulsion, and repetition that secretly hold the energy and vitality of the essence experience. Addiction strikes fast. From the first high, the dream gets externalized. For example, one original dream essence is alcohol. Essence of alcohol vs. addiction to alcohol: alcohol the archetype vs. alcohol the addiction. The essence dream carrying the archetypal energy is always on the periphery. With alcohol it's simple. When Rob started drinking scotch, he felt wonderful. Shy and self-conscious in social situations, he suddenly felt confident, strong, alive, and full of words. "Hear me, see me, feel me," he demanded.

The difference between the archetype and the addiction is the pure spontaneous energy of the "scotch" as against the ritualized orchestrated daily use of alcohol and the dramas of going from pole to pole that emerged. Patti, a forty-three-year-old woman looks for the nurturing mother she never had. That is her complex, a cluster of dramas, behaviors, beliefs, and repetitions organized around the mother archetype. Patti, stuck in the labyrinth of the complex, yearns for the archetype, the unadulterated, pure energy of Mother.

Another example is Alex, whose early sexual, sexualized fantasy and ritual brought him calmness every time, secretly accessing his own archetypal natural flow in himself, in the other, in the world? Recently, Alex has been complaining of depression and the tendency to give up.

Asked to recall the feelings and energy of his calmness, Alex makes a gesture, holding both hands, above his chest, straight up and open. Everything is OK. Then he assumes a gesture indicating his depression and tendency to give up. He lowers his hands so that they fall limp at his sides. These two positions, the hands up and open and the hands falling limp, facing down at his sides, indicate polar opposite positions. Ironically, one is determined by the other. The more depressed Alex gets, the more calmness is secretly present. The more calm he is, the more depression is hovering. The big secret is that these poles are actually a continuum of energy. Why is calmness such an extreme pole? Because the dream of calmness, the experience of OKness that appeared spontaneously with the "first high" experience is pure archetypal energy. There are no vessel, no earth, and no mirror to sustain its circuitry.

How do we bring these two fixed states, calmness and depression, to their essence-continuum? These are the underlying assumptions behind this work: 1) that the two gestures and postures are accurate portrayals of his underlying feelings, that Alex's subjective experience should be valued and trusted; 2) that movement, which is not present in the two fixed positions, is a valuable, unoccupied channel where the continuum between the two extremes may be experienced; and 3) that within this polarity there is essence.

First, Alex assumes his calmness posture. Then (without thinking) Alex goes into his depressive posture. At first, the back-and-forth postures occur slowly. Encouraged, he slows down even more, moving back and forth between the two positions. Suddenly Alex starts to talk. He's reached an edge. Stopping his movements completely, Alex says, "I'm lost." Sensing that now Alex is no longer held by his rational mind, he is encouraged to not think at all and go back into his back-and-forth postures even more quickly. Alex starts to go back and forth even faster. He is encouraged to speed up, and he does. He moves faster and faster until he is going back and forth on his own, with no memory of the instructions. As he finds his own speed, he begins to smile. Grinning from ear to ear, then smirking, then grinning from ear to ear again. What is the name for this experience? "Joy."

As you can imagine, the atmosphere that Alex grew up in held no permission for joy. Ironically, the fragment calmness and the fragment depression add up to the essence "joy." It is "joy" that secretly drove the experience of calmness as well as the experience of depression. How can Alex live joy, use it consciously, bring it to his work, his relationships, his daily world tasks? How can he bring joy to his body and to the problems or conflicts that befall him? Now that its truth has been experienced, doesn't this create an extra burden? Would it be a better choice to have left this essence in the background? Now that it's here, and has been reexperienced, it's always a choice. The days in the Garden of Eden, where all desires were instantly gratified, are left behind. And, remember, without awareness, we revert to sleep. Even in the midst of totality.

That's Alex's dilemma, as it is for all of us. That is the work that is alluded to after Adam's sin: staying awake, working, seeing oneness in dual opposites, seeing your problem as a vessel for returning to essence.

Supposing that you don't do that, nature will do it for you. Essence is compelled to be realized. If it cannot be expressed face-to-face, openly, without distortion, it will be expressed in its fragmented form: symptomatically, disturbingly, painfully, and with suffering. We cannot avoid suffering. The only question is whether we are willing to experience our fate on a heavenly level, in our active imagination, or on a physical level. It's the difference between the process of actually dying versus dying-into-life. The desire, the essence, seeks expression in every cell of our being. Your inferior function will always create problems, opportunities for this growth. The original problem is always pushing you to be everything you can be.

Late in life, Carl Jung gave a talk in a church and upon leaving, had an argument with the deacon. When accused by the deacon of repeating his "father material," Jung said, in effect, that these things are never finished, that they come around even many years later to push you into something new. That's why the dream-gate of alcohol is always there for an alcoholic.

Jimmy, a sixty-year-old recovering alcoholic, complained of his inability to consummate deals. He feels unworthy, inadequate, and makes no impact on his clients, though he is excellent at "getting the ball rolling." He remembers drinking beer in high school, but that his first great high came from drinking vodka martinis in college. So cool, so sophisticated, so confident, vodka martinis cut right through Jimmy's innate shyness. Confidence ruled. Suddenly Jimmy became the center of attention.

Everybody loved Jimmy. He was a magnet. Jimmy became a successful advertising and marketing executive using this capacity. Without vodka, Jimmy reverted to being the isolated, depressed, inadequate person of his childhood. Now sixty and abstinent from alcohol for eighteen years, Jimmy finds himself in a situation where he still needs to make a living and also prepare for a possible retirement. He's overwhelmed and has never developed or incorporated the state of confidence, vitality, and adequacy with others that the vodka incarnated.

Jimmy recalls the feeling of the vodka, the sense of aliveness, the lack of self-consciousness, the enjoyment of being with people, meeting them, talking to them, learning about them. As he speaks about his experience, his body starts to move and his hands join in expression. Bringing out the movements even more, Jimmy's hands and arms start to make ever-larger circles. Following his movements, Jimmy says, "This feels like when Zorba the Greek begins his dance and brings everybody in." Happiness all over.

Jimmy doesn't realize that he brightens every doorway he enters. That's what vodka does for Jimmy. He forgot or never realized that the vodka is really him. That's the dream behind his current problem: for Jimmy to use his Zorba-like essence in his day-to-day professional life, in his salesmanship, and in his communication. The other problem with reexperiencing and using these unbridled energies is that, without awareness, and without detachment, they overwhelm us and make us drunk. How does Jimmy use his Zorba energies without getting drunk on them?

One way is for him to bring in his day-to-day person: low-energy, no confidence, no enjoyment. A posture that holds Zorba's energy is like Jimmy standing tall, with his hands pointed upwards, his eyes closed, in the ecstasy of the moment. In his current, day-to-day identity, Jimmy assumes a bent-over, slumped, head-down position. Gravity pulls him. This is the perfect juxtaposition to his state of ecstasy, and the perfect addition to complete Jimmy, the perfect brake, an earthly vessel to his personal heaven.

What does vodka-Zorba look like before he became so big that it made Jimmy drunk? What does the lackluster, day-to-day Jimmy look like before It became so big that it made him sick? Are these two extremes secretly one continuum? Jimmy begins to play with both postures. Going back and forth until he can't tell the difference, Jimmy finds an elegant dance and movement that reminds him of Fred Astaire. That elegance, grace, and ease, is very inviting, alive, relaxed and aware.

Jimmy's missing essence was fragmented into the extremes of one that looks like Zorba, the other like a humbled old man. Every addiction carries an essence that is trying to happen, that got fragmented sometime in life. That's why addiction can be a fast track to wholeness when the process is made conscious and experiences are trusted. Jimmy's Fred Astaire elegance, energy, and persona are exactly what he needs for making friends and influencing people.

The choice is always whether to drink the vodka outside oneself or retrieve your own essence from within. That's why the impulse to drink always brings the possibility of joining the dream and living from its essence. This parallels reidentifying with the essence uncorrupted archetype rather than falling and crashing into the magnet of the complex where the essence energy and behavior live in distorted shadow version.

For example, Jimmy spent a lifetime looking for the father. His own father, a successful alcoholic professional, was depressed and unavailable most of the time. Vodka held the dream and experience of Jimmy's masculine vitality, spirit, and judgment. The addiction, the behaviors, mindset, rituals, and dependence on alcohol and its relationships, relying on drinking alcohol rather than relying on its essence, result in an inevitable loss of esteem for being a slave to something outside yourself, not carrying permission for your own desire and ability to take for yourself; this is the complex. Retrieve the archetype, retrieve the essence. The problem is always a dream gate to your essence. Alcohol, the drink, is the problem; the alcohol archetype that Jimmy experiences as Fred Astaire is the solution. Every first high brings the reality of permission. Real desire, unmirrored, becomes shame. Our instinct for actualizing who we are becomes thwarted. The mirror we expect, the mother and father imprinted in us, has inadequate reflection. Socialization denies other desires. Each society or tribe dictates which beliefs and behaviors are acceptable. Our instinct for survival takes over fast. Essence is never lost. Instead, it remains camouflaged in distorted forms. A face turned backward is a metaphor that describes essence energy that remains present but subdued in a secret façade. Just as "religion is a defense against religious experience" (Carl Jung) so, too, addiction is a defense against its essence.

All the time Jimmy spent in bars, all the money lost when the alcohol didn't work anymore and he started drinking for the sake of drinking, all this occurs when alcohol becomes the end rather than the means of accessing the initial dream. Permission is the "holy grail": the realization that you're here to receive, that you're here to become everything that you can be, that the purpose of creation and nature is to realize your path. But the first high skips the scenic route that you must take to realize when you're off track. Instant wholeness is not earned, it's a theft in the night. Its experience overwhelms the rational. But its experience remains, forever imprinted and pushing to be realized and identified with.

Dylan is a thirty-two-year-old male who has difficulty expressing anger and complaining that something is wrong. His girlfriend criticizes him in a way that intentionally elicits an angry response. When he finally shows his anger, she responds by smiling. She seems to enjoy this pas de deux that connects Dylan to his anger and its expression. Dylan dreams that as he's leaving a place that he visited with his mother he must close the gate, which requires him to fit the two latches of the gate perfectly. As he starts to do this, his mother jumps in and tries to do it herself. Dylan yells, "No," with all the rage of his being. What is the essence of this rage before it became so big and so secret that it must be hidden? Is it simply a matter of his being afraid of his anger? Does the dream reflect a point of frustration between Dylan and his mother where he has never taken his power or had it validated by her? We know that the dream presents a potential Big Dylan that is the sum of enraged Dylan and his critical mother. Enraged Dylan plus a critical, impatient mother equals essence. When Dylan's rage is amplified, Dylan stands tall with fists held up and he shakes with rage. Encouraged to stay with his anger, to hold his fists and shake even more and pay attention, he suddenly looks up in realization. "I feel I don't need to look and apologize for living. I can do what I want without regard for what anybody else thinks." Dylan now looks relaxed and in a state of grace: "I have permission." Now Dylan can follow his heart.

Permission and following his heart is an essence whose fragments are an enraged Dylan plus his critical mother. This essence is his adult. And when he doesn't identify and live from this larger Dylan, the fragmented version of this essence rules again. The dream behind every addiction holds the instinct for permission and acceptance. The first high restores this nature, a reawakening of our natural desire to receive and its permission. Stuck in a mother complex, Dylan is miserable, and in the reflex and insult of constant criticism and a lack of self-acceptance, he perceives that something is chronically wrong with him. His essence experience of "permission" is the unadulterated restoration of the Feminine archetype to Dylan. Tana, forty-seven, identifies herself as an adult child of an alcoholic. She never puts herself first. Her entire life has been devoted to the needs of others. Since she precociously anticipated her father's and mother's needs, taking preemptive action that saved the day, she has been consumed with the well-being of others while sacrificing her own desires, needs, and dreams. Tiring of this role, she recently has become depressed. The energy for "fixing others" is gone. She is encouraged by her family and friends to think of herself for a change, but she gets even more depressed by the pressure for her to have any expectations and desires for herself. Expert in anticipating everybody else's needs, she's completely unable to identify her own.

Every time Tana meets somebody, she immediately relates to their injury. The secret addiction here is that "I'm whole and you're broken." But the broken pole of this deal has now broken through Tana's awareness and has become her new identity. She's the broken one now, depressed and in pain. Like Dylan's dream, Tana is the sum of both her OKness and her brokenness.

Tana demonstrates her OKness (how she feels when she's relating to a broken person) by holding her hands with her palms straight up, indicating "everything is OK. I'm OK. You're OK. Everything feels perfect. I'm calm, very relaxed, very in control. Just the way I should be." Now, the other pole: depression. For Tana, depression feels lifeless. "I feel like giving up." Tana brings her hands to her sides, holding them limp. Tana starts with her hand up in OK position, then drops her hands down to depressed position, then back to OK position. Repeating the cycle, she comes to a point where her self-consciousness takes a back seat. Starting slowly, the movement between the two positions increases in intensity. She's encouraged to speed up. She stops and says: "I wonder where this is all going." Tana had hit an edge. First acknowledging her resistance to go further, Tana then goes back to the movement, encouraged to go even faster. Then she smiles. She keeps going just to verify that she's actually feeling what she's feeling. What's the name of this feeling? Tana says, "It's laughter." Essence "laughter" is the dream behind Tana's codependence. Living from laughter is so foreign to her. She does not remember an experience of laughing. Laughter brings the permission for Tana to live. In fact, it skips the middle-man of permission because it is permission itself. The imprinted Mother and Father archetype are encompassed in Tana's laughter and ready to be lived. Since the Garden of Eden, living from essence requires the work of awareness. Otherwise, our tendency is to go to sleep and revert to living in its shadow. Permission brings the visceral experience of Tana's larger Self, guiding, being, more aware, more inclusive, more loving, more mature nature.

When therapy is based on a disease or medical model, the presenting problem has a locus that must be identified and destroyed. Seeing an addiction or behavior as a defense to overcome or as an illusion misses the natural process that is trying to happen: that the problem before you in its current outer form is secretly essence waiting to be unfolded. The disturbing problem brings the process right to your doorstep. The disturbance spiritually synchronized with nature's strive for wholeness is your own personal Tao. To experience the answer from within is the quest of our times. Coaching and interpretations are the Band-Aids of civilization.

Personal truth must be experienced. Coaching someone to overcome their problem, complex, or addiction without processing what is trying to happen, basically ensures that the unprocessed polarity remains status quo, that the other side will come back with a vengeance or find an even more dangerous form of expression or symptom.

A psychologist was happy to report that his patient dreamt that she vomited out her cocaine. He thought his treatment was working. Now strong, she was ridding herself of her poisonous contaminant and returning to her unadulterated self. This would be healthy if the cocaine in the dream was the powder that she put in her nose. But the dream cocaine carries much more than its literal image. Remember, every part of the dream is "you." Vomiting cocaine is the equivalent of disavowing an essential part of herself. That feeling, that experience, that energy, that permission, that desire felt in the first great experience with cocaine now looks like cocaine. Tana's internal image of cocaine carries this whole-making part, exactly what is missing from her day-to-day identity. Vomiting the cocaine means that this remains outside of her. She feels safe. Nothing has changed.

Identifying with this bigger facet of one's self seems very dangerous and unknown. Accepting completion from within entails sacrificing the greatest illusion ever held: that everything good exists outside. The truth is that our connection lies within and our job is to include all the fragments of our experience: good and bad, weak and strong, holy and evil, to realize that we are their sum.

CHAPTER 11

REALationships

At birth, a baby has an innate sense of its potential. Endowed in archetype, then nourished or thwarted by the dominant caregiver, the child develops a sense of self: is she/he an active child, a verbal child, a quiet child? Responded to, or not, the initial self, which is natural to the child, is either encouraged or neglected. The developed self, "true" or "untrue" to its nature, becomes the basis of personality. A person may then recognize his or her own self for what it is, or, overshadowed by an unresponsive environment, forgo that and become what she/he has been seen to be in the eyes of "the other." This underlies whether a person becomes part of a relationship or REALationship in the years to come. That is the focus of this chapter.

Like seeks like. But that's not how we operate. Many books, many hours, many lifetimes are spent on seeing oneself through the other. Instinctively, we expect a mirror. Like a heat-seeking missile, we know the existence of this mirror because it's imprinted in us and waiting for a place to happen, to actualize in day-to-day reality. We seek the other looking for what is missing in us, that which in the other completes us.

Initially, we put forth our best. And it was rejected. Now, expert at what is secretly missing, we see a vision of completeness and OK-ness with the other. Alone, we remain broken. That's our fate, to be wandering eternally in a diaspora looking for wholeness, looking for home. This complex and repetitive addiction secretly holds our biggest essence, the same essence guiding force that drives all of nature, life, and creation. What essence?

Pharaoh decreed that all the Israelite men must leave their wives and live in the work camps. Cohabitation was outlawed. The continuity of a people would be stopped. Their fate sealed, all seemed lost. But, the women brought their mirrors. Finding the men in their work-camps, each wife took out her mirror, held it up to reflect her face and said, "I am the most beautiful creature in the universe." Then, handing the mirror to her man, he looked at his own reflection in the mirror and spontaneously said: "I am the most beautiful creature in the universe." You might think that the woman, healing the wound of her mate, would say, "You are the most beautiful creature in the world," but her mate's Big "I," is within him and not his wife. His wholeness is his mirrored state. In the face of disaster, they prospered and multiplied, able to steer a course that chose life and avoided certain annihilation. That strength, that guide, that skill, that wisdom, that conscious awareness, that permission for life manifests in mirrored reflection.

The essence reflected is "I," a state of being that can be in two or more worlds, two or more realities at the same time. Imagine, if those women, seeing their broken husbands, told them how beautiful they were without a mirror. Their wholeness would have remained in the image of the other and dependent. No "I." What "I" are we talking about? The "I" of self-love? Self-esteem? Self-aggrandizement? Self-importance? Self-promotion? Self-survival? All the small selves that dominate our culture, the narcissism we glorify and are either too proud of or secretly use in the service of power? Where power rules, love is the outsider. No. This "I" is our essence "I." We have an image of ourselves, our possibilities and destiny: Individuation, our bigger nature, striving to be revealed, organizing purposeful events, tendencies, challenges, and problems congruent with our search for meaning. Many images, myths, and stories in our culture exemplify this journey. What you won't find is an image of a couple in a relationship. Couples are hard to find. The couples we know, the ones driven by love, are tragic: Romeo and Juliet, Caesar and Cleopatra, Tristan and Isolde, and on and on. Love kills. In contemporary peoples' dreams there are very few images of a relationship couple.

What is a relationship couple? Two people that fit together, that form a "we," in a bond of love. Not a love in enmeshment, not a secret partnership where each completes the other, not a secret exploitative use of the other for self-completion, not a collectively driven need to fit in, but two adults, responsible for themselves, in conscious partnership. The dream of relationship is so powerful as to render us totally vulnerable to anyone who comes to us with the offer of finding it. Every problem and symptom, unfolded, will bring you to the gate of relationship. The process never stops at the boundary of the individual. Expressions of insight, feeling, understanding, mastery, power, and real desire remain incomplete without relationship. Like kundalini energy rising from the base of the spine, every process reaches the chakra of relationship. The energy will get stuck or appear as symptom unless identified, accepted, and used.

So many behaviors imitate relationship. Since the dawn of civilization, gossip has been a norm. We share gossip and talk about another as if they are out there, a powerful ghost exerting forces on us, somehow worthy of our judgment, our disdain, our conspiracy. We party together in an orgy of gossip all around, point fingers, accuse. The problem is that who we gossip about, that ghost that's supposed to be out there somewhere, is not local—it's secretly us. That disgusting husband, that unscrupulous colleague, that flirtatious wife, that tyrannical boss, that impossible mother, that depressed friend, that hyperactive child, that unforgiving brother, that selfish neighbor, is all "you!"

Gossip exists in overt pseudo-intimacy with others. But no relationship exists, with the others or within your self. The relationship channel is closed. Without relationship, there is no unity. That's the ancient idea of leprosy. When you gossip about others, you disavow that part of yourself that represents the gossip's target. Without awareness, we earmark ourselves for the very destruction we seek for others. We offend nature. Our exclusion sets off a chain reaction that does not stop at our door. We reap what we sow.

The intrigue, the vengeance, is the hit. Involving others, the behavior takes a form that appears as relationship. But the process is self-serving and secretly gratifying. Are we shamed? That we have to steal? Consciously, no. This feels pretty good. It's a high to be part of a mob, to be included; having the power of inclusion or rejection parallels judgment over life and death. Losing connection to our instinctual need for diversity creates tyranny and offends nature.

Ellen has known Rhonda for forty years. They first met at a mutual friend's house. Both Ellen and Rhonda have kept their connection to each other throughout. As both women grew older, Rhonda became aware that Ellen disturbs her. Finding Ellen in her presence, Rhonda becomes anxious, feels like she wants to flee.

Rhonda says Ellen is a constant, mean-spirited gossip. "When she isn't besmirching others, she constantly speaks about her material wealth. There is a series of broken promises and commitments, with no awareness or acknowledgement of the impact on me." When Rhonda confronts her friend, Ellen always has an excuse. She never says she's sorry. Feeling abused and ignored, Rhonda tells Ellen, "I no longer am your friend. It's taken me a long time to make this decision. Now that I've made it I'm sticking to it. Don't call me. I will not return your call. Good-bye."

Ronda says, "As I get older I realize my time is limited. It's not that I think of death. It's rather that I think of life and how I want to live it. Every day becomes more and more precious. Friends, family are getting sick: some have died. I want to spend my time with exactly who I want to be with, not Ellen. It took me a while to get there, but I'm here. I'm relieved." So, what has been the purpose of Rhonda's long-term relationship with Ellen? A few possibilities:

1. Rhonda needed Ellen to find her own strength, to tell her truth and end the relationship.
2. Rhonda is lonely and desperate for friendship.
3. Rhonda believed that if she stayed a consistently true and good friend, Ellen would change.
4. Rhonda could not accept the reality of her friend's betrayals. Rhonda disavows her own capacity for betrayal.
5. Rhonda vicariously enjoyed and was awed by Ellen's behavior and wealth.
6. Rhonda was so intimidated by Ellen that she would never confront her.
7. Rhonda was secretly gratified by convincing Ellen that she liked her and pretending that all was good.
8. Rhonda felt Ellen would protect her if she needed it.

Breaking up today is seen as a rite of passage. It's easy to break up and see the other as the problem. But the break-up itself doesn't break the trance. Leaving a friend, lover, husband, or wife without finding what held you together in the first place keeps you the same, ready for the next repetition.

When Rhonda imagines Ellen, the thing Rhonda immediately notices is Ellen's dark hair falling into her face. Rhonda immediately associates this with heavy mud, and she feels disgust. She grimaces and says a very emphatic "yuk!" Rhonda recalls her first experience of feeling that way: A young child in a doctor's office, recovering from an operation, the doctor smiling, walking toward her smiling. Little Rhonda looks at him and knows that he will hurt her. Ellen equals "yuk." "Yuk" equals inevitable pain from a betrayer wearing a helper's mask.

Every experience has a direction. For Rhonda, "yuk" has a distinct energy that resonates when she walks east. How does Rhonda find this direction? Rhonda takes a few steps in every direction and finds the one direction that feels right, that is the one with the energy of "yuk" in it. Only one direction is right. East. Taking a few steps east, Rhonda stops. Another vital aspect is ready to surface. Who in Rhonda needs to see this mud, witness this "yuk?" Rhonda briefly closes her eyes and says, "It's the young child who was about to be hurt." Now Rhonda starts to experiment with the different directions that are congruent with the energy and sense of that child. It is south. From the point where she stopped going east ("yuk"), she now takes a few steps south and stops. Rhonda winds up at a point directly southeast of her starting point. By walking these directions, she has added/included/combined the child with the "yuk." Going back to the starting point and walking southeast, Rhonda experiences lightness, peace, and a sense of well-being.

To the participants, to the rational mind, we have two people, one annoyed and the other annoying without any deep and purposeful meaning, or any truths revealed, except that it may be time to move on and give up this fantasy. But "home" is the hibernating essence. We look for home. We know it's there. How ironic that the antithesis of home, Ellen/"yuk," holds one of its components. The disturbing relationship always manifests the polarity of a fragmented essence, two seemingly exclusive and unrelated worlds that compel inclusion. For Rhonda, "home" is her essence, her natural wholeness, her love and heart, her path of least action where everything seems natural. Now the experienced essence "home" is the guide. But that disturbing direction of

Ellen is also a guide. An awakened distinction and sense that now exists between walking the path of "home" that feels so right and walking the path of "yuk," that sidetracks. For Rhonda, the relationship with Ellen brings her to her essence.

In a Russian fairy tale the young prince catches a glimpse of his beloved just as she sails off. He embarks on a journey to find her. He enters the deep forest seeking the Baba Yaga, the awesome witch-goddess of nature who resides outside the civilized sphere, to ask her where to find his beloved. As he approaches, he notices that the Baba's house marks a different space and energy: the house rests on chicken legs and is in constant motion. Like all sacred spaces, time meets eternity, the bush burns but isn't consumed, walking on water is a reality, and opposites don't nullify each other. This space encompasses being in two or more realities at the same time.

When he asks where to find his beloved, Baba responds: "Are you doing this for yourself or by compulsion?" Another way of asking this would be "Are you doing this for yourself or for somebody else?" The prince faces the dilemma of answering the goddess. If he answers that he is doing it for himself, she will kill him. If he answers that he is doing it by compulsion, she will kill him. And she is a goddess, so if he lies, she will kill him. What, then, is an acceptable answer? What would you answer? The prince answers that he is doing it two-thirds for himself and one-third by compulsion. Identifying with both, his request is granted. By including both opposites, he transforms.

What does the prince's answer have to do with Rhonda? Consciousness requires being in two places at the same time. Real here-and-now existence requires a tension of opposites and consciousness of polarity. Big truth encompasses duality, dialogue, inquiry, polarity, contradiction, paradox, absurdity, humor. There needs to be somebody home watching the store. Ironically, when you are the sum of the watcher and the store, the magical third force, your essence, is restored. The circuit between the seemingly unrelated poles connects. Essence restored and redeemed, the connection to Self. We're born as fire, full of archetypal essence, energy forms that are complete, unified, universal, instinctually driven to actualize, to live. Realization of an instinctually triggering archetype requires mirroring, a reflection from others, from those around or from the environment. We expect this reflection. It should be there. We know it's there. And, when we don't get it, we're shamed. The mirrored experience does not occur. In a flash, something is wrong. With us. Nature's energy, our endowment, projects outside ourselves, in the other, or it goes into our background to reemerge symptomatically as fate. Compelled to be expressed, this energy dreams its realization with or without our conscious participation and won't be denied. Its shadow will do. Its distortion in complex will do. Its death side. Its power side. Its tyrannical side. Its trickster side. Its ecstatic side. Its destructive side. Its chaotic side. Its cowardly side. Its psychosis. Its hubris. The archetype continues to be expressed, even in shadow form.

Behind relationship lies that initial moment of unmirrored rejection and nonrealization, instinctual betrayal of our most fundamental expectation. Most relationships are determined by the story and fragmentation of Self born of that moment.

Going back to the prince, there are two ways he can search for his beloved:

1. The frenzied search from inadequacy and incompleteness that seeks what is missing from and through the other.
2. The search from the heart, from real desire, from love.

Remember when Pharaoh prohibited the men from living with the women? The women brought mirrors. Gazing at their own reflection, they saw the most beautiful creature in the universe. The story continues with the men taking the mirrors, gazing at themselves and seeing the most beautiful creature in the universe. Suppose the men skipped this step? Isn't one whole person enough for two? No. That initial shame remains determinant. Partnership requires two complete people. The men would not have realized their own "I." When the prince answers Baba Yaga, "two-thirds for myself, one-third by compulsion," he enters that special mirrored space where the rational mind no longer rules. A death takes place—of the ordinary and familiar, of the story, of the conversation. Real relationship between two complete people is a special club. To join, death is required.

Mickey and Rosalyn have been friends for twenty-seven years. Despite their individual history of marriage, divorce, betrayal, frustration, fulfillment, and growth, their friendship remains. While each bears witness to the other, they have themselves grown. Initially, they met in group and formed a friendship based on a kindred spiritual quest for the Self. They knew and understood each other in that way and rooted for each other to find meaning, direction, and emancipation. However friendly they were, a relationship/partnership between the two of them was always dismissed. Why? It was understood and agreed: the sexual attraction was not there for either of them. Neither party fit the other's image of their sexual mate, neither felt attracted by the other's shadow.

Suddenly, that changed. Rosalyn worked hard on herself and, with much sacrifice, found her bigger Self, her larger nature. More quiet, more detached, more aware, more confident, more adult, for the first time she began to live distinct from her tragic, repetitive story. Simultaneously, Mickey had been working on himself. The coup de grace was a car accident. After the accident, Mickey noticed a much slower awareness, a stillness, within. Mickey started to operate from that stillness and to rely on its slower pace. He was more alive, awake, and earth-bound. When he found himself to be exhausted, Mickey would go to that stillness and revitalize. One day, exhausted, he noticed his body's tendency to drop. Paying attention, noticing the body as it dropped into a couch, he decided to slow the drop down so he could experience what was happening. Suddenly, on the way down, he came to a posture where the exhaustion was gone, where lightness and ease took over. He found that special place through exhaustion. Disturbing exhaustion brought him back to his place of effortless stillness, where he was awake, alive, feeling.

Beginning as two incompatible people, though friends, they suddenly found each other. Here's why: The problem with our bigger Self, our higher Self, is that its presence is missing. The reason we search is that we desire what was once there. Its lasting impression fuels our yearning. Our own wholeness pushes and tugs at us, in the dream of the magical other, in our envy of others, in our magical addictions, in our thefts, in the narcissism of depression where we think, "I'm responsible." There is wholeness out there. Maybe not for me, but it's there. Without our bigger Self, we live in shadow. Nothing is real. Realities remain separate. Awareness has no vessel, there is no choice. Every activity follows its own inertia. A feeling is a fact.

Earth symbolizes the vessel. Our biggest nature, our essence, our ally, needs to land. Otherwise, we are stuck floating in this universe alone, desperately seeking completion through the other. Mickey and Rosalyn now relate from their bigger nature, not their "story."

What is it like to operate from your essence? Bob is a corrections officer. He asks, "What is the difference between passion and essence?" Passion, by itself, is energy that has no vessel, fire unharnessed. Bob said, "As I was processing a new inmate, he ran away and was resistant. The other officers subdued him and brought him back. When it came time to bring him to his bed, he ran away again. This time, the other officers were determined to teach him a painful lesson. Envision the paperwork. Envision the effort. Envision the mess."

Bob took the prisoner by the hand and brought him right to his bed. How did he know that was the right action? The missing expression? "I can't explain it, I just know. When I do that, that's essence, not passion." Essence is easy—it's the least action, direct, a feeling of being very awake and aware, or life being full of many possibilities. One action feels right. One direction, one action, one movement, one sound almost self-expresses. Caught in opposites, the Center of the moment, the point of real action is found. It seems easy, effortless, because all of nature is behind it.

So, *passion*, as Bob called it, is only one pole of a polarity. The other pole might look indifferent, unfeeling, having no desire. Essence is the sum, dance, inclusion, combination of passion and its opposite. The practice of inclusion of these opposite worlds recreates perception. Essence-level perception is more earth-based, detached, and heartfelt. Feeling and relating require detachment, as do staying awake and consciously participating. Essence-level perception includes these attributes. In relationship, imagine yourself with your own personal ally who is with you, who helps guide and protect you, who accepts you as you are. So light, so easy, compared to being transfixed in expectation of the other to fulfill a dream. Imagine the resentments that don't get played out, the misperceptions that don't get acted out when each individual brings their own permission for life and fulfillment and the heart is able to express itself unencumbered.

A relationship between two or more people also carries its own essence. In the background of conflict and diverse behaviors, an essence prevails. Each behavior is a fragment of an existing totality that has always been there, that drives the action. What does this look like?

First, intimacy. Modern man and woman: we are wounded. But the dream of intimacy and realization of joining remains the instigator and organizer of our attempts.

Love requires heroism and warriorship. Intimacy is not for the faint-of-heart. Intimacy is the special Sabbath, a hidden valley whose entrance is scary to those of us who have been wounded by rejection of our initial, instinctually driven foray into this land. There is a point of desperation and fear at the dream-gate of intimacy and at the boundary of every process that takes us outside our "box." The experience seems intolerable. Just below our radar, the disturbing terror of the new has already been resolved, usually with behaviors or repetitive actions—sure things that nullify the disturbance. We beat the system, and don't let ourselves in on it. We survive. Ferociously and ruthlessly, we abandon the dream. In the fire of survival, we do anything—the ultimate "fuck it." Every problem brings us to a moment of choice where this drama prevails. Whether it's the point of using cocaine or the risk of intimacy and love. The irony is that the very fire of survival that secretly guards the status quo is the very fire of survival that you need to identify with, to gamble everything for love. Even if you die. The same ferocious ruthlessness that keeps you in your "story" is the same ferocious ruthlessness that needs to be identified with and consciously used.

A biblical example: Moses battling Amalek. Moses holds his hands to the heavens and gets support for his arms from the entire community in his battle. Amalek and Moses, a battle of equals, except that Moses is connected to higher purpose and is supported by the whole community. Connecting to the infinite source, Moses's arms uplifted symbolize the Self-ego connection. Moses prevails.

Following Christ's process, the task is to "die," consciously and voluntarily. Death leads to resurrection. Intimacy requires such a death experience. Every time we use our ruthless and ferocious nature with awareness, every time we stay with the disturbing experience, we die into a new reality. If you do this, why would you be with someone who doesn't come from the same experience, who takes no risk, who is still stuck in her/his story, where love and heart stay on the periphery?

When Vera, thirty-one, first glanced at Alex, she saw the most handsome man she had ever seen. She knew she was staring but couldn't stop. First he glanced back. Then he noticed her stare and approached her: "Are you new around here? You must be, or else I would have noticed you." Vera could not breathe. Words clogged in her throat would not come out. She never expected him to even be aware that she was alive. Their first date, an ordinary movie, put her on a high. He walked her home, holding her hand. She tingled all over. His good-night kiss was fire. Alone in bed, her body ached.

They started dating. She told her best friend about the wonder of it all. Her best friend looked uneasy. Vera thought that it might be because this friend wasn't seeing anybody at the time. Vera then turned to another close friend to share her exciting experience with Alex. The other friend revealed that Alex had been having an intimate relationship with Vera's best friend throughout. Distraught, Vera confronted Alex, cried hysterically, and then accepted his fervent denials. They got married. Twenty years later, this story recycles. In fact, Vera is scheduled for her next distraught episode as we speak. Rehearsed in his denials, Alex has no qualms.

Vera is educated, professional, and literate. Over the past twenty years both Vera and Alex have seen several counselors, at her instigation. Nothing changes. Her friends and advisors recommend leaving him. Why does she stay? Why does she participate in this story's reenactment? Isn't repeating the same actions and expecting different results insane? Coming to that point of desperation, anger, and fear is also the point of re-enacting the drama. You identify with desperation but do not identify with the ferocious nature behind keeping things the way they are. That distinct ferocity that takes over and repeats the same scenario as if it had never happened before contains the person's hidden strength. At the point of repetition, whether a food-addict grabbing a carb, a cocaine addict grabbing a snort, or a woman victimized by a cheating man, is the most powerful force of our nature. The question is on what side do we use this strength?

As was stated, the biblical parallel to our own dilemma is the fight between Amalek and Moses in the book of Exodus. Three days after the Israelites reached the highest level of consciousness, the fiftieth gate, while crossing the red sea, Amalek attacks. He is that aspect in us that always attacks and sends us back to our Egypt. Egypt is our fate — our death, our off-track. In choosing Egypt, we value safety and survival over love, heart, and truth. The important image from the story is that only when Moses is able to hold his arms up to the heavens does he prevail. Like Moses, we cannot defeat the embedded script of our survival without connecting and trusting a higher intention.

Vera needs her conscious ferocity to do battle with her secret ferocity. Is she willing to be as ferocious in pursuit of her freedom? Or will she revert to the safety of her predetermined "story?" Up until now, Vera enlisted numerous experts overtly to reconcile with her husband but secretly to overpower him. Now, the point of desperation and pain brings her to a confrontation with the Self. No Self. No "I." No Me.

Real relationship, intimacy, and love require two "I's." Both must bring their own ferocity. Ironically, the dream gate to these individuations, the ferocious nature that each individual soul needs to be fully present, awake, and available for intimacy, lie at the point of recycling. They contain the secret strength of the person; the same "fuck it" that returns you to the trauma is the same "fuck it" that sets you free. Is Vera ready for this spiritual encounter? Is Alex really her problem? What happens if Vera does battle with herself and realizes her own strength and independence? If she starts to realize her own independence, how will Alex react? Is it possible that, in Alex's behavior, lies a similar dream for his own individuation? Can the relationship survive with two independent persons who operate from the heart rather than their story?

What can happen in a situation like this is that one partner will realize the other is not the problem — they're just doing their job. At that point, they become aware of their own dream and their own desire, which has always existed until it was obscured by their smaller story. Sometimes their partners grow with them. Often they don't. What about Vera? She has decided to concentrate on her work as a relationship coach who glorifies the sanctity of marriage. Not trusting her crises as an opportunity for her own growth, she prefers to bask in the fantasy her marriage affords her.

Of course, Alex hasn't changed a bit, but neither has the fantasy. The fantasy holds the dream, like Eden. So much of what happens when people get together is about this fantasy. Women, usually, are driven by an image centered around being together, around family, and around being taken care of and protected. Men are caught in sexually fulfilling images and expectations. These overlap, but the mortal day-to-day truth of being with the other is inevitably disappointing when measured against the dream. It's the dream that remains constant. The reality is referenced by the dream. The dream remains the determiner of the way people feel about themselves, about their place in the world, about their worth.

Absent her fantasy of marriage to Alex, Vera does not feel life is worth living. By pretending that everything is okay, Vera stays glued to her dream and never has to face her inevitable loss.

Alex lives a different version of the same deal. By living his sexual fantasy with others and then returning to the devastated, hurt, and mortal Vera, he, like Vera, returns to a wounded pairing, a party of tears. They are two pained and dependent children who need each other to exist and hate each other for it. Vera's retribution comes in the form of acting as if she's okay, coaching relationships, her chosen profession, as if she's an expert in her own.

Alex's behavior has often been associated with Don Juan and Peter Pan, two eternal youthful males of no responsibility who never come down to earth and its daily drudgery or suffer the wound of being in an intimate relationship with someone who impacts them. These princes are nothing without their fellow princesses. Vera, by living her lie, is inviting death. Both partners have a contract to avoid death at any cost; that's what binds them. There's nothing that is going to change this until one of the parties wants more. This is an example of a couple where each participant's drama brings them to the doorstep of their own individuation. Except that, at the point of the drama where each member has a chance to say "no" and break the drama, they choose to repeat.

But the drama always takes them to the precipice of their own journey. So Vera and Alex's "we" may actually be two separate "me"s, where each, on their own, can be OK without the other. While their destiny may be to be apart, fate keeps them together. Like many contemporary couples, a dream of independent completeness and adequacy realization may be what brought them together. Everybody has their own time frame. But the dream of completeness starts with our birth. Our essence is both imprinted and experienced. We know it's supposed to be there. Unmirrored, it then lives in projection outward, in compartmentalized secrecy and in fragmented archetypal dramas.

The following is a sequence of how this dream takes different forms in a lifetime, ultimately finding itself in relationship.

Starting at age five, Rudi found what he was looking for. Moving into a new neighborhood, he immediately noticed the vitality, the smell, and the clothes of the young mothers in his area, quite an antidote to his own depressed and world-beaten mother. The moment these women walked by all was perfect. Rudi said that he once read a description of a fetish where the author said "It might be something as simple as getting an erection upon seeing a woman's shoe." Rudi said that this doesn't describe the experience. It's not *an* erection, it's *the* erection. Rudi created a fantasy around these women. By age eight, he could masturbate to orgasm around the image. By eleven, he could ejaculate to this image. He relied on his secret fantasy as his main resource to cope with his frustrations and challenges. The state he would always get to in his fantasy ritual was "warm relaxation." A lot of drama and fragments went into this warm relaxation, but the fantasy was one-hundred percent reliable and the resulting relaxation was everything. In a way, everything else besides the fantasy images took second position to this addiction. After all, warm relaxation meant everything, even if it meant keeping it a secret and living in the shame of inadequacy, wholeness being experienced outside the self. Relative to the outer hunt for goddess females who fit the image of the fantasy, virtually all other activities took second position. "If your car has eight cylinders, two are for daily life. Eight, you save for the goddess." The dream of warmth, the actual experience of warmth requires the image of the adequate one added to the image of the defective one. Added together, in unconscious, ritualized drama, the essence of warmth is reexperienced but never identified with or owned.

The dream of warmth then found its milieu in relationship. Choosing a partner who looked very adequate and together on the outside but was secretly very hurt on the inside, Rudi found a fellow traveler to share his dream of warmth in relationship. Both members now projected their warmth outside themselves. Neither the relationship nor the image of the other party would hold the dream of warmth for very long.

Divorcing after twenty years of marriage, Rudi developed type II diabetes, which is marked by insulin resistance, that is, the cells refuse the body's own insulin, resulting in elevated levels of sugar that destroy the body's organs. The process at hand is an inability to receive the natural flow of existing insulin.

The oldest Judaic-Christian tradition is oneness. All the different manifestations of God and nature are the force of God. The universal intention behind these forces is what brings oneness to the vast diverse and oppositional faces of the divine that the ancient world personified as gods and goddesses. Oneness is essence. The problem befalling you seems antithetical to oneness, like an illusion that must be repudiated or a cancer that must be removed. But the problem is actually notifying you of God's presence, an opportunity to follow the Tao, which is to bring the action that's occurring in any part of the body to the light of day, to every part. That's how you experience the dream and synchronicity between that part of the body and all of you. The Tao is where the action is; that's where God is, that's what's trying to happen, in the moment. That's the opportunity for reentering the dream. That's our time. Rudi's local experience of diabetic symptoms is really not local and is secretly occurring in every part of Rudi. That's why healing, as well as disease, is contagious because it's going on everywhere. Its compartmentalization is what keeps us sick. The process and dream that's trying to occur cannot be erased by eliminating one of its symptoms in one or two body parts.

Rudi's dream of warmth initially presented in a goddess fantasy. Then it traveled to relationship, and subsequently to diabetes. Rudi imagines seeing his insulin receptors bracing, strong, and determined to hold back anything. Then actually demonstrating the energy of the bracing, Rudi holds out his arms in protective stance, completely still, fists clenched. Holding that position, he exclaims that "This reminds me of when I arm-wrestled. I wasn't very strong, I couldn't beat anybody, but, in this position, nobody ever got me down." Reenacting this arm wrestle, identifying his right hand as "him" and his left as his "adversary," Rudi suddenly realized that he was "pulling in" as well as "pushing out." Rudi was taken aback that the secret of his strength was in "pulling in" as well as "pushing out." As Rudi continued to practice his new capacity, "pulling in," he realized that he wasn't aware of who or what is receiving what he's "pulling in." So pulling in combined with pushing out is at the edge, the gate, of receiving.

But Rudi was without conscious awareness or memory of what it feels like to receive. His early goddess fantasy and his brief experience of warmth from his marital relationship are so secret, even from himself, that he has no inkling that he repetitively evokes this experience of warmth every time he indulges in his goddess fantasy. Warmth is receiving. Rudi doesn't have a clue. Suggesting that Rudi just follow his body, he says "Maybe I should cut off my head." A perfect idea. Rudi imagines placing his head in a pail and lies down. Then we wait to see what the body sans head wants to do. The body starts to move, then gets up and walks. The walk becomes hard, stomping the ground.

Encouraged to continue and follow what he's doing, Rudi keeps walking and stomps louder. Perfectly comfortable, Rudi walks like this and stomps for ten minutes. No extra energy is required. "I could do this forever," says Rudi, "but am I pissed. My body doesn't need me. I'm insulted and rejected. I'm fuckin' furious. I'm also devastated. Not needed." This feeling of rejection, of not being needed, is the new edge to receiving and just being in the experience of the Self, in the experience of the essence warmth essence, receiving and just being. Rudi is devastated. The rational mind has taken over. The experience of just being, letting go and letting nature take over is very threatening. Recall the story of Swami Kripalu who fell into the Ganges, got caught in the current, and found himself drowning. Suddenly, a voice said, "Let go. Stop thrashing. Let the current take you." That saved his life. At one time, our thrashing saved us. Initially, it contained the fire of our survival. Now, just the form remains. A momentary Center, thrashing is now an empty form that makes us sick. The new Center is the "letting go."

An individual consumed by his/her survival thrashing is not available for relationship. Only a pretense of "we" that actually includes another person at the heart level can exist. Two people who bring their own awareness may enter a gate of relationship and intimacy. This must be done consciously—entering relationship with no awareness always leaves stragglers behind. Somebody in us is always left back, the hurt one, the angry one, the shy one, the panicked one, the one who lives in the terror of the initial rejection. Without a conscious gate, our hearts are not included. The sum of all of us brings the heart. A deep democracy is required.

The idea isn't one hundred percent agreement. It's acceptance of every part. It is inclusion of every diversity. It's a mindset of acceptance rather than exclusion, an inner consensus that values every part. Without this mindset, the opening for relationship will be missed. A pseudo-version that imitates the dream but is predicated on the fantasies and inevitable disappointment of two thrashers is always the available path, the path without choice.

Returning to Rudi, at the boundary of intimacy between himself and Vera is the same identity crisis that parallels his insulin reception, the cauldron of destruction if he follows his nature to be, to follow his heart, to connect, to feel, to be felt. Does Vera reciprocate? To date, Vera's alliances have always reenacted looking for the father and finding men who either acted out their neediness or acted out their distant unavailability. They are both seduced, both familiar, both safe.

But Vera has worked on herself and has shared her fear of intimacy with Rudi. Both fear letting go and being consumed. A mythical obligatory, devouring, and enslaving dragon lies at the gate of relationship, choice, and participation. Rumi said, "Gamble everything for love." That's what it takes. Going over the edge consciously, taking yourself with you, noticing all the way. No secret alliance or enmeshment. Seeing the other as they are rather than how they're supposed to be. Seeing yourself as you are, eyes open, accepting yourself, accepting the other. We must stay with the tension of awareness and not fall into the familiar. "Gamble" implies a risk, an effort, a task, a choice, and trust that the process, that nature, has a purpose and an end. That process is love. The process is heart. That channel is relationship. Is love possible? Is sex where both parties stay awake and aware of each other possible without reverting to the sure thing, being swept off your feet, ecstatic fantasies, expectations, stories, and disappointments that originally made life possible to endure, to secretly enjoy, to beat fate?

Rudi and Vera, with beginner's minds, choose to go into their no-man's land of being together, feeling together, touching each other, and tasting each other, staying awake, noticing and trusting each experience as it comes up. The impulse to beat fate for each member is to revert to the intoxicating certainty of their own secret story, reenact the secret hit that solves the eternal wound of their existence even for a few seconds. The realization of relationship is sacrificing that act out and staying with the experience at hand. So far Rudi and Vera are devoted to this realization and gamble all for love.

Going from object to feeling, Rudi and Vera start to participate and experience each other. No longer hunting each other down in measurement of their suitability to fit each other's fantasy image, they witness their own feelings and reactions. Their energy flows outward in realization of their instinct and desire in the world with another person, their consciousness synchronized with the permission and awareness of an inner experience of an "I" that now must seek expression with an actual other.

CHAPTER 12

Conclusion

Jung found that the dream that is trying to happen continues day and night, personality development proceeding at the unconscious level. The goal is to become as complete a human being as personal circumstances allow. How do we do this in our time? By turning inward, encountering that personality and that energy that seems most disturbing. Similar to descending into the underworld, it is there, in the disturbance, that solutions are found. Stepping into the darkness, you step into life as it can be lived. You may, as Jung experienced, be blessed with a "creative illness," a time when you are convinced that all is lost, that you are beyond help. Socially isolated and doomed, you are actually at the door to your natural path, which all of nature supports. Experiencing Self, one is here for the first time, more consciously present and more alive then ever before.

Self is experienced whenever a disturbing, alien energy is joined, accepted, and incorporated. Personality spontaneously transforms. Insight is gained. New perspective is born from the important truth of realizing that what is happening to you has meaning and that these energies, truths, and perspectives compel inclusion in every aspect of life, in every modality of expression, in every type of relationship. Now each of us can participate in the process formerly reserved for mystics, prophets, philosophers, and poets by embracing problems and symptoms as guideposts organized by Self. Knowing your psychological type, you can now honor those types that are not comfortable for you: the introvert steeped in an inward movement of interest away from the outer world; her/his counterpart, the extravert's interest in the outer world. You can expect that the problems of your life will occur primarily in your inferior, uncomfortable function.

When couples carry their partner's shadow, the image of the other holding this energy stays until the other can redeem it. Redemption takes place when one steps out of time, out of rational thinking and survival, accepting the energy of the other as their own. Recently, a man in his sixties experienced a full blown panic disorder triggered by an episode of suffocating. The manifested panic was the secret trauma that he had always hidden: on the periphery of his consciousness, the secret, helpless, vulnerable child who could not make it in this world. This time he stayed with the energy, visualized staying with the child while he experienced his fright. It took three weeks of work but the panic lifted and in its place, this energy, now joined and incorporated, brought the vitality and excitement of that boy into the stream of life. To the provisional ego it looks like panic; now lived, it is the lightness of being, the excitement of life.

Most medication and intervention would cement the shadow of that traumatized child forever by recreating the same polarity between the traumatized child and the one who acts adequate. One or the other, the adequate one now requiring ever increasing medication to sustain its power. But by embracing the shadow, the hurt child, its archetypal energy is now transformed and redeemed. "This is the best I've ever felt. When I was twenty, I felt like eighty."

This lifelong process of growing into yourself is called individuation, a living presence in each of us bringing precious meaning and direction to life, your true Self. How do we promote our unconscious to realize itself? By noticing, by examining what is expressing, by what is flirting for your attention, by what is compelling you to notice. This Self realization requires one's psyche to turn around on itself, reflect on itself and confront what it has produced. In this awareness, you may experience yourself as split in two: you as the mortal person struggling to survive, and you, the unconscious other, manifesting in personalities, powers, moods, and opinions forced on you, Self energies demanding your attention or making you drunk.

What happens then? You develop heightened consciousness and recognize your psyche is a living, real, objective entity. As you age you become the sum of all your shadow integrations, an accumulation of Big "I's." As you become the sum of all these energies, Self actualizes: you earn wisdom, and get along with all kinds of people, including yourself. Deepening your own democracy, you accept your own diversity. Rather than petrifying, aging brings a realization of your full potential, a progressive normalizing of your own natural order. The crucial question is, are we related to something infinite or not? Are you aware that the infinite, the eternal, the imperishable is ever-present in yourself? Despite its appearing to be hidden, Self is the bedrock of all reality. As Jung experienced and expressed it, the great secret is to embody something essential in our lives. Then, regardless of age, we can proceed with dignity and meaning.

For Jung, the major theme in life is the mystery of opposites: their division, their union, their transcendence, and the cosmic significance held for human consciousness. Bringing those opposites to their oneness restores our connection to our natural essence. Jung saw the journey of personal development as lining up these opposites and holding their tension as the path underlying the higher consciousness that exists in eternity. Our psyches, existing as a part of nature, contain the same law that governs the universe. You fulfill the requirements of that law through the miracle of consciousness. The human psyche provides the mirror in which nature sees herself reflected.

For Jung, the highest state of consciousness becomes yours when you embody Self; its goal being wholeness, it holds the blueprint for human existence. Seeking fulfillment in the spiritual achievements of art and religion, it also seeks it in the inner life of the soul, which we experience in the images of dreams, in the problems of our existence, in the symptoms that we create, and in the dilemmas that we find ourselves in. When these outer representations are noticed and taken seriously, we join Self. Ego realigns to its source. Tao returns. Is Self another word for God? Yes, especially when your most disturbing problems take Center stage. It is then that you know that Self is instigating your transformation from lead to gold, and the gold is you.

About the Authors

Marcella Bakur Weiner, Ph.D., is a fellow of the American Psychological Association (APA) and an adjunct professor of psychology at Marymount Manhattan College, New York City. Weiner is president of the Mapleton-Midwood Community Mental Health Center, a treatment center for community-living residents. Prior to her current pursuits, she served as senior research scientist for the New York State Department of Mental Hygiene, where she published seventy-five articles. On faculty for the Institute for Human Relations Laboratory Training, Weiner has trained professionals in the United States and overseas, including in China, Japan, Cuba, Switzerland, Thailand, Greece, Turkey, and Egypt. She is the author of and contributor to twenty-three books.

Mark B. Simmons, LCSW-CSWR, is a trained Jungian analyst specializing in the treatment of addictions and second half of life processes. His approach combines Jungian depth psychology with Kabbalistic knowledge and principles. He is currently codirector of Amaury, a nonprofit foundation providing training, seminars, and clinical supervision of treatment based on the work of Carl Jung. A supervising analyst, lecturer, and trainer, Simmons currently serves as consultant to Managed Care as both program consultant and educator in providing alternative approaches to the treatment of addictions. He maintains a private, spiritually based practice in New York City.